Charisma

The Art
of
Relationships

Michael Grinder
Author of *The Elusive Obvious* and
Managing Groups—The Fast Track

with Sharon Sayler and Mary Yenik

Acknowledgments

I sincerely thank the whole village for sharing their talents in critiquing, expanding, revising and producing this work:

Steve Andreas, Michael Anvick, Rachel Babbs, Rachel Beohm, Nancy Blackwell, Cynthia Blix, Kathy Burke, Nancy Burns, John Cleary, Steve Cowie, Tim Dalmau, Theresa David, Calvin Dettloff, Krista Dettloff, Mr. Dogs, Gabriele Dolke, Rebecca Drury, Pat Duran, Fleur Easom, Kathleen Epperson, Amanda Gore, Gail Grinder, Lety Gutierrez-Shelly, Linda Haines, Paul Henderson, Becky Herndon, Rosalind Kingsmill, Susan Krohn, Barbara and Michael Lawson, Dee Lindenberger, Hazel-Ann Lorkins, Karen Masterson, Ian McDermott, Barbara McIntyre, Seth Morris, Carol Mulcahy, Rick Mullins, K. N. Padmantohan, Joyce Patterson, Jane Peterson, Gary Phillips, Richard Quatier, Kevin Quinn, Linda Reed, Eric Richards, Carolyn Rosard, Ron Sangalang, Adam Sayler, Sharon Sayler, Rudolf Schulte-Pelkum, Bill Sommers, Sarah Spilman, Stephanie Staley, John Steinberg, Nancy Stout, Ashton Thomas, Kathryn Wainwright, Pavita Walker, Buck West, Ya Ya Sisters of the Royal Exchange, Mary Yonek, Mary Yenik, Kendall Zoller and Steve Zuieback.

Editors and Conceptual Collaborators: Mary Yenik and Sharon Sayler

We thank Ashton Thomas for his contribution of *Don't Read This Book.*

Cover Design and Layout Assistance: Sharon Sayler, webmaster@michaelgrinder.com

Desktop Publishing: Stout Graphics, Nancy Stout, nk-stout@comcast.net

Screen Savers: Stephanie Staley

Technical Support: Adam Sayler

Second Edition Proof Reader: Rudolf Schulte-Pelkum

Third Edition: Consultant and Editor, Philippa Pride

ISBN-10: 1-883407-10-9; ISBN-13: 978-1-883407-10-0

Copies of **Charisma—The Art of Relationships** can be purchased directly from:
Michael Grinder & Associates
16303 NE 259th Street
Battle Ground, WA 98604
(360) 687-3238; FAX (360) 687-0595
Website: http://www.michaelgrinder.com

Second Edition 2006

Third Edition 2009

Fourth Edition 2014

Dedication

This book is a cat and dog analogy. It is about behavioral styles. One style seeks to please others and another style answers only to oneself. This book is about balancing ourselves with both styles; it's about having areas where we are one style and areas where we are the other style.

My wife Gail provides that balance for me. My world makes sense because of her unconditional acceptance of me. Her love balances my professional world where fame and failure are equal imposters. Because of her support, I operate as if I have insights that others want. And yet as I drive home and press the number one button on the cell phone, a voice answers that melts my cat-like assertiveness to puppy love… and I begin my weekly courting of her. Gail's even temperament makes her our family's emotional North Star.

My wondering how I provide a balance for her was answered during a recent fight in our office. Our voices were escalating when the business line rang. Switching to her innate sweet voice, she competently handled a request for a product. Hanging up the phone, I teased with, "How come you don't talk to me like that when we're fighting?" Her response confirmed my value, "Because you are the safest person in my world."

Preface

Are you a cat or dog?

Don't read this book! Did this statement challenge you? Did you arch an eyebrow and become somewhat indignant? Are you innately drawn to that which is "off-limits?" These are cat traits described in this book.

Did you feel confused by the statement? Did you want to comply and put down the book? Did you have the urge to move on to other reading materials? (We actually do want you to read this book.) These are dog traits.

These two reactions of *intrigue* and *compliance* illustrate, in a broad stroke, the concept behind *Charisma: The Art of Relationships*. Relationships are the key to leadership, morale and productivity. Knowing how to recognize whether an individual operates more as a dog or more as a cat allows us to select the appropriate strategies to foster and maintain a relationship with that individual.

Charisma is based on the fact that each of us has a cat and a dog part. In certain situations it is appropriate to increase our cat-like behaviors and in other situations we want to increase our dog-like behaviors. We want to master more than the science of getting along with others. We want the art of accessing our own and others' strengths.

By applying the analogy of human behaviors to a house cat, we show the effectiveness of intriguing the cat personality. It is best to develop a relationship with a cat indirectly. A cat will turn up his nose and snub that which is presented directly to him. Yet, the bowl of food or treat that is put on the top shelf will suddenly become the cat's target of curiosity. And, while the cat will often have no time for the affable dog, he may miss important contributions that the dog has to offer.

Likewise, people can act like (hu)man's best friend—always wanting to satisfy others. And when others are not happy, the dog presumes it is something he did. He resolves to try even harder to please. Dogs like clarity—it is best to develop a relationship with them directly and openly. While the dog wants to get along with the confident cat, his desire to please irritates the cat even more. He misses being seen as valuable. The dog needs to increase his range of flexibility.

THIS is why everyone should read this book. It is more than a clever comparison between our behavior and that of our favorite animal counterparts. By extending the comparison, *Charisma—The Art of Relationships* finds its true value. By modifying our own behaviors we create our own success through relationships. And in so doing we influence the groups in which we participate.

So, to you dogs who have made it this far: I encourage you to keep reading. *Charisma* will give you an improved understanding of bothersome cats that seem inflexible or overly indulgent. You will be pleasantly surprised at the techniques' effectiveness in one-on-one relationships as well as relationships in a group setting.

And to the cats out there: well, you're going to do what you want anyway, you will know best whether you want to miss a book that is worthy of your challenge; an opportunity to understand the differences between being a leader and being a *charismatic* leader.

Table of Contents

How to Use This Book

There is no magic, only magicians.

As a company, Michael Grinder and Associates is committed to reversing the trend of over-training/entertaining and under-implementing. To assist you in learning the skills in this book, the following features are included:

- **Shadow box.** The key sayings are in shadow boxes. Some readers like to surf pages to read the shadow boxes. Then when an idea intrigues them, they read the full text.

- **Vignettes.** Many of us learn best through stories. These are boxed and shown in a different font. Some readers will jump to them and when engaged will then read the text; others will read the text and use the vignettes for reinforcements. The Index lists the vignettes by title.

I-1

- **Free Worksheets.** All of the major concepts of the book are formatted into easy-to-use worksheets. These forms allow the reader the opportunity to practice the skills. A worksheet is indicated by a CD icon in the margin. The first number indicates the chapter followed by the worksheet number. For example, I-1 indicates Introduction, first worksheet. The free worksheets are located on our website (www.michaelgrinder.com).

- **Free Screensavers.** We are all very busy and yet want to continue to professionally grow. Screensavers address this need. When our computers are at rest, the concepts appear on the screen with an attractive background. The page reference is listed to encourage us to further extend our learning. Free downloads available at www.michaelgrinder.com.

- **As a learner** (practice exercises). When you see the symbol of a runner, you are encouraged to engage in the learning activity. Reading this book and not doing the exercises is fine—it will increase your cognitive competence and allow you to understand cats and dogs. The practice exercises will increase your behavioral competence. So both the cognitive and behavioral readers are welcome and the latter will profit even more.

If practicing a skill with another person isn't practical, there are several other options:

- Visualize: When have you noticed this skill in the past? When would you want to use this skill? When might you notice this skill in the future?

- Plan: With whom would you want to role-play this skill?

Each of us has aspects of being catlike and doglike. Ideally, the cat in you will be ambitious and want immediately to be charismatic. The dog in you will provide the persistence in learning the skills needed to become charismatic.

- **DVD and Audio CD Set.** Spend an entertaining 90 minutes with Michael as he relates his cat and dog analogy to everyday life. The skills are simple, practical, and immediately useful. Topics include understanding how to manage difficult personalities, increasing the efficiency of committee meetings, developing presentation skills and raising teenagers. Michael's engaging style, humorous anecdotes and poignant insights will have you both laughing and reflecting at the same time. To purchase, go to www.michaelgrinder.com

Introduction

Charisma is the ability to
influence through relationships.

There are many degrees of charisma. Most of us don't really want to lounge on a Tahitian beach and paint.[1] We want to have enough influence to insure that our work is meaningful and to come home to family and friends. Others of us hold positions where we directly influence the atmosphere in which others toil. All of us are affected by relationships and by our own and others' style of leadership.

I-1

Why are some people easy to form relationships with and to work with while others are not? Often, the difficult person to work with is the "power" person who is the linchpin to the much-needed team collaboration and cooperation. Charisma is most evidenced when strong people willingly follow. *Charisma—The Art of Relationships* offers a non-judgmental way to understand these power people (they are usually cats) and it provides strategies to bring them aboard. The vehicle to these strategies is the analogy of cats and dogs.

Anyone who has ever owned a cat and a dog instinctively knows the differences between their personalities. By examining people as if they are cats and dogs, we transfer our intuitive knowledge of animals to people. Even Dilbert, in his capturing the cubical life, has the evil director labeled "Catbert" and the gentle consultant named "Dogbert."

I-2

One way to think about the differences between relationships with cats and dogs is to consider their *degree of accommodation*. When you call a dog it comes; when you call a cat, its machine takes a message and the cat gets back to you later—maybe.

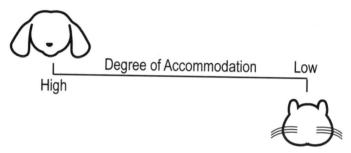

Exercise: Think of people who are high accommodators… the people who always help, support and assist. In our personal world these are the friends and relatives that want to bring a dish to the party and want to stay after to wash the dishes. And of course, they send you a "thank you" note.

At work, these people nod their heads when we offer an idea or suggestion. They are the ones that send us congratulatory emails when we have an accomplishment, even a small one. They offer to join committees such as the "sunshine committee."

> *When a person feeds a dog,*
> *the dog looks around and says to himself,*
> *"Wow! You provide me shelter and care for*
> *my every need. You must be a god."*[2]

Another way of describing cats and dogs is to use a different continuum—degree of independence.

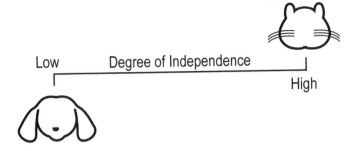

Low   Degree of Independence
                                          High

Exercise: Think of people who are high on the independence scale... the people who always dare, push the envelope and risk. In our personal world these are the friends and relatives that feel insulted if they are not invited to the party but don't want to commit to attend. And it wouldn't occur to them to phone if they are going to be late. Late? What's late? I can still grace them with my presence!"

At work these people are not known as good listeners—unless they are learning something that they can massage into their own idea five minutes after someone else initiated the idea. They are unaware of protocol and hierarchical structure. They fully embody the concept of, "It is easier to do something and see if anyone in power notices than to falsely humble oneself by asking permission."

> *When a pet owner feeds a cat, the animal looks around and says, "Wow! You provide me shelter and care for my every need. I must be a god!"[3]*

Vignette: Dead Sea Scrolls Poem[4]

It is reported that the following part of the Book of Genesis was discovered in the Dead Sea Scrolls. If authentic, it would shed light on the question, "Where do pets come from?"

And Adam said, "Lord, when I was in the garden, you walked with me everyday. Now I do not see you anymore. I am lonesome here and it is difficult for me to remember how much you love me."

And God said, "No problem! I will create a companion for you that will be with you forever and who will be a reflection of my love for you so that you will know I love you, even when you cannot see me. Regardless of how selfish and childish and unlovable you may be, this new companion will accept you as you are and will love you as I do, in spite of yourself."

And God created a new animal to be a companion for Adam. And it was a good animal. And God was pleased.

And the new animal was pleased to be with Adam and he wagged his tail. And Adam said, "But Lord, I have already named all the animals in the Kingdom and all the good names are taken and I cannot think of a name for this new animal."

And God said, "No problem! Because I have created this new animal to be a reflection of my love for you, his name will be a reflection of my own name, and you will call him DOG."

And Dog lived with Adam and was a companion to him and loved him. And Adam was comforted. And God was pleased. And Dog was content and wagged his tail.

After a while, it came to pass that Adam's guardian

angel came to the Lord and said, "Lord, Adam has become filled with pride. He struts and preens like a peacock and he believes he is worthy of adoration. Dog has indeed taught him that he is loved, but no one has taught him humility."

And the Lord said, "No problem! I will create for him a companion who will be with him forever and who will see him as he is. The companion will remind him of his limitations, so he will know that he is not always worthy of adoration."

And God created CAT to be a companion to Adam. And Cat would not obey Adam.

And when Adam gazed into Cat's eyes, he was reminded that he was not the Supreme Being. And Adam learned humility.

And God was pleased. And Adam was greatly improved.

And Cat did not care one way or the other.

Benefits

I-3

By increasing our understanding of ourselves and others, we build a better foundation of communication. And by realizing our own tendencies, we recognize when we can be ourselves and when we need to be flexible.

The benefit of applying our common understanding of cats and dogs to people is that we become more realistic and respectful in our expectations of ourselves and others. We have practical strategies for forming and maintaining relationships with a wide variety of people. We don't expect a "cat" person to be easy to influence and manage, just as we don't expect a "dog" person to be assertive. This work will result in:

- Understanding ourselves and others

- Accepting ourselves and others

- Understanding how our and others' "catness" and "dogness" are situational

- Separating our and others' intentions from actions

- Interpreting our and others' behaviors more accurately

- Enticing cats to be cooperative

- Providing new ideas on resolving conflict

- Knowing which conflicts not to try to resolve

- Managing difficult personalities

- Luring a cat to see the benefits of being a team member

- Improving our leadership to attract more cats

- Understanding cultural differences

> *When picking a pet, keep in mind that*
> *to a dog, you're family;*
> *to a cat, you're staff.*[5]

Cautions

This work is about behavioral descriptions of people. Humans are more complex than models that describe them. I have never met just a cat person or just a dog person. The terms cat and dog are used to simplify the message and to make it easy for us to see the contrast. Categorizing people as cats or dogs would be incomplete without three cautions.

First Caution: Context

The first caution is that a person may behave differently in different contexts. For example, an individual might be a cat at work and a dog at home.

Vignette: Context

Jordan is an upper middle manager. He conscientiously arrives at the factory 30 minutes before anyone else. He finds the silence precious—a time to think and preview the day. Finishing his cup of coffee, clipboard with the day's schedule in hand, he is alert and ready as the staff arrives. He is proud of his high position of responsibility at work.

His evenings and weekends are his sanctuary with his spouse. He has resisted the temptation to sign up for committees at church. This year he even decreased the amount of Christmas decorations he normally puts up. He loves his low-level of responsibility at home.

Mary Beth has a college degree and a teaching credential; however she is a teacher's assistant. While she only makes a third of the money she could, she is very content to follow what her lead teacher wants her to do. Mary Beth cares about the kids and does a fine day's work. And yet she likes the fact that she doesn't carry a satchel of work out to her car.

Mary Beth's greatest object of caring is her family. She is very ambitious for her husband and children. Her evenings are spent listening to everyone's daily adventures. She volunteers to scan the Internet for information that her husband needs. She relishes her nightly ritual of sitting with her learning disabled daughter when the clock strikes "time for homework." When Mary Beth's head hits the pillow she knows she has given her greatest love and attention to her family.

Vignette: Situational

The concept "situational" extends to animals as well as people. A police officer with a trained canine is visiting a school. The children love touching the dog. The officer is called to duty and warns the children to stay clear of the dog as the dog enters the car. The transformation is a huge surprise; as the dog enters the back seat, she bares teeth and growls furiously. She has been stabbed several times while encountering suspects.

Second Caution: Expectations

The second caution refers to your personal expectations of what are cat-like behaviors and what are dog-like behaviors. These expectations come from the culture to which you are accustomed. For example, if an individual comes from a family of cats and is the most accommodating member, then the individual sees themself as dog-like. However, the individual's coworkers may very well see that individual as a cat. Be aware that your view of cat-like and dog-like behaviors might be very different from that of the next person.

Vignette Expectations

Renaldo was raised in New York City and proud of it. He loved the rush of energy needed to compete. Whether it was how fast he could walk the 20 blocks to school, or who watched the most weekend TV football games, or who could talk the fastest, Renaldo was ready to compete. He earned his nickname of "Rushing Renaldo." His habit of bettering the other person served him well until, in his mid thirties, he was transferred to a small town in the Southern part of the US. In this slower-paced community, Renaldo had a hard time falling asleep at night. He missed the constant din of the night and he knew that somehow he was "off" at work.

After being on the job for three months, his supervisor, Billy Ray, sat Renaldo down. Billy Ray started the conversation with, "I have relatives in New York City. When I visit them, I have to gear myself up for the faster-paced life style. I have to remind myself that when they don't respond to my questions but instead switch topics, they don't intentionally mean to insult me. When I meet my family's new friends, they will think I am not as bright as they are because I don't talk as fast as them. Those people I have met and spent time with on previous visits have moved beyond the prejudice that 'speed of voice is equated with intelligence.'

Here, people have the reverse prejudice of New Yorkers. They mistakenly interpret your fast speaking pattern as slick and not genuine. Your subordinates want to follow your directives but they also want to be clear about what you want; because they perceive you as impatient, they may be hesitating to ask you clarifying questions. Figure out a way for them to be comfortable enough to approach you. Your peers will trust you much more after they get to know you, so you may want to accept some of their invitations to socialize with them outside of work. Your superiors will need to reflect on your suggestions, so put them in writing. That way, they have more quiet time to think."

When Renaldo shared his learning with his wife Gina that night, they were able to understand the cultural differences between here and "home." They both pledged to support each other in carving out a "home" here in the South.

3rd Caution—Comparison

The third caution has to do with how cat-like or dog-like I am compared to people around me. I can be myself on two different committees. On the first committee, most members operate from their cats. I am seen as patient, a good listener and peacemaker. On the second committee, most members operate from their dogs. I am seen as driven, opinionated, goal-oriented. I haven't changed; it's just that I am in a different context.

Vignette: Time with People

I am blessed to have a multifaceted life. On the Myers-Briggs personality model I am an extreme introvert. I crave the quietness of my acreage and physically working with my hands. At the same time, I make my living being in service to people. I live in the greatest neighborhood I have ever been connected with. We are always there for each other and yet we give each other privacy. Professionally, I am surrounded with very bright, well-intentioned associates—Nancy, Mary, Sharon, Gary, Kendall, Adam. And I have a wide range of friends.

Sharon has taught me that "time is the most precious coin that we spend." How I spend my social time is critical to my well-being. When I have been on the road too much, I just want to mentally close the gate to the property and hibernate. When I am in my writing mode, I want to be around friends and associates who will challenge me. Their "cat" pushes my "cat." They force me to examine and rethink my lines of thought. During this phase I don't need "yes" people. And yet, when I have been challenged by life, I want to be around people who accept and emotionally cradle me. My "dog" needs to be cared for by their "dog."

I have diverse people in my world. I am being myself when I am around them. How I appear is based on my cat-like / dog-like behaviors compared to their cat-like / dog-like behaviors. How I am is relative to how they are.

As we have established, everyone has a part of them that is a cat and a part of them that is a dog. Charisma is the ability to recognize which part of you is called for. For example, there is a part of us that wants to follow the rules and a part of us that wants to be creative and not follow the rules. The question is when to "bake like a dog" (follow the recipe) and when to "cook like a cat" (be creative).

> *Cook like a cat; bake like a dog.*

Exercise: Reflect on the Three Cautions

First Caution—Context.

Context includes your roles at work, at home, as a parent, as a spouse, as a sibling, as a neighbor. It also includes your finances, learning, romance, gardening, cooking, sports, board games, spiritual matters, vacations, and ambition. In which contexts are you most cat-like? Where are you most independent from others both in terms of not needing them or being concerned how they see you? In which contexts are you most dog-like? Where are you most dependent on others both in terms of needing them or being concerned with how they see you?

Second Caution—Expectations.

Often our expectations come from childhood. How does the country / region where you were raised influence how you see cat-like and dog-like behaviors? How does your family of origin influence your view? At different ages have you changed your view of what are acceptable behaviors? In Chapter One a short genealogy is offered for your reflection.

Third Caution—Comparisons

Sometimes, being around cats brings out my cat. And other times, being around cats brings out my dog. The same is true for being around dogs. Which set of people are most cat-like in my world? Which set of people are most dog-like in my world? Which people tend to elicit my cat-like behaviors? Which people tend to elicit my dog-like behaviors?

Chapter One: My Pet Tag

1-1

"Cats & Dogs" is not a personality model.
It is a behavioral model of communication.

Personality models operate on the basis that people are the same apart from circumstances. I am impressed and have profited from personality models—notably Myers-Briggs and DISC.

Cats and Dogs is a behavioral model rather than a personality model. I have a part of me that is an independent cat and a part of me that is an accommodating dog. The secret is to know when and how to access which part of me.

Vignette: Writing a Book vs. Carrying out the Trash

When I sit down at the computer to work on a manuscript, I want to be in my cat. Being arrogant gives me confidence, "Ah—the world needs these pearls of wisdom." I operate with the goal of packaging concepts that will be helpful to others. The sense that my understanding is worthwhile and will make communication more successful for others is a much-needed impetus to write.

If I sat down as a dog, my internal dialogue would be, "Who am I to offer anything? There are so many other people who are smarter, more experienced and more insightful than I am." My humbleness restricts my flow of ideas. I am stymied by my own view of myself compared to other people. All the liabilities of my dyslexia are activated.

Gail is living proof that the title of "domestic engineer" is an apt description of a real set complex skills. I reap the benefits of her relaxed manner in planning meals, caring for our family and slating our social activities. My dog part readily accepts all of my assigned roles.

The one consistent pattern that I have to be aware of is when I have been on the road doing a series of one-day workshops to large groups. To do well in front of large groups, I access my cat. If I come into the home still in my cat, I unconsciously strut in as if to say, "You are so lucky to be with me!" "You want me to take out the trash? Me? I just spoke to hundreds of people this past week." I have to switch from my cat to my dog before I come through the back door...and take out the trash.

1-2

When are you more cat and when are you more dog? The questionnaire on page 15 will help you identify the circumstances that draw out your dog or cat. A copy of it can be downloaded from www.michaelgrinder. com. Select only the items that pertain to what you are reflecting on. This and other worksheets are intended to be used several times.

Since the categories of cat and dog are relative, reflect on a relationship or context where you are more cat-like. Then reflect on a relationship or context where you are more dog-like.

Insert "I" or "I am" in front the appropriate description. For example, "I am more confident than competency warrants," or "I am more competent than confident."

Questionnaire

Category	Description of my cat tendencies	Description of my dog tendencies
Confidence/ competency	__more confident than competency warrants	__more competent than confident
Operate	__from my position as the pilot	__from my person as the flight attendant
Voice pattern	__credible	__approachable
Aware of other animals	__not very aware of dogs	__much more aware of cats
Power	__comfortable with it	__shy from it
Seek	__promotion / challenge	__comfort
Conflict	__don't back away __often unaware if I cause the conflict	__frightened and confused by it __offended if I have to point out something
Innate traits	__ambitious	__vulnerable
	__just being myself	__very aware of others
Average trait	__want to be respected	__want to be liked
Extreme trait	__arrogant/martinet	__guilt-ridden /sycophant
When stressed	__seen as angry	__seen as pleading / victim
When calm	__seen as definitive	__seen as seeking information
People	__hold accountable	__highly accepting
Emphasis	__issues	__morale/relationship
Management style	__intervene early	__intervene much later
Gestures	__palms down	__palms up
Level of influence	__greater influence	__lesser influence
Self image	__self select; from internal	__dependent on how others see
Perfection	__motivated by progress	__love doing the same activity that satisfied others over and over
As parents	__assure my children that they are someone	__encourage my children that they can be someone
Purpose in life	__to dabble and tinker	__to be happy
New things	__if select it, am very excited	__want to do things well
Intrigue vs. Clarity	__love intrigue	__love clarity
Apology	__What are you talking about!	__will initiate even when not at fault
Learning levels	__drawn to and inspired by complex skills	__polish old skills and master new skills
Decision-making process	__love to decide	__would rather only gather info

1-3

Origins of My Self-Image

Our self-image is formed from our family and school social life. Our expectations of what are cat-like behaviors and what are dog-like behaviors are based on the culture we come from or are in. Our self-image often stays with us even when the circumstances of reality change. For example, if we come from a family of cats and we were the most accommodating member, our self-image is that of a dog. However, we may very well be seen by working colleagues as a cat.

To further discover the origins of your self-image, review your immediate genealogy. Often our expectations of ourselves are inherited—inherited in that we respond to the models we were raised with. (We thank Fleur Easom for creating this chart.)

Put the appropriate letter next to your parents and grandparents:

- a lowercase "c" if the person was somewhat of a cat

- a capital "C" if the person was definitely a cat

- a lowercase "d" if the person was somewhat of a dog

- a capital "D" if the person was definitely a dog

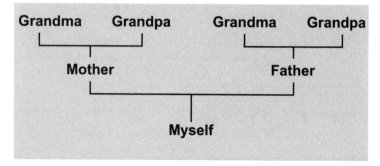

Next, put the appropriate symbol next to your parents and grandparents:

1-4

- a "+" if you interpret/perceive the display of the person's cat/dog traits as positive

- a "-" if you interpret/perceive the display of the person's cat/dog traits as negative.

Based on the above information, how is your self-image influenced?

Is there a correlation between gender and expectations of how to behave? Would the "+" and "-" have been assigned differently if the person had been the opposite gender?

> *Our self-image is the number one variable that influences our professional growth.*

Position and Person Axes

1-5

There is a part of me that is my person and a part that is my position. My individual personality and my position have to be compatible.

In order to understand where we fit on the cat and dog continuum, let's assume the term *position* is interchangeable with cat and *person* is synonymous with dog. The advantage of adding position and person to our vocabulary is that we increase our ability to predict when we are likely to switch either from our position to our person or the reverse.

1-6

Sometimes "burnout" is when I have too high a position for my personality. Another way of saying this is, "Not enough cat for the job and the levels of responsibility that accompany the position." How I handle tension is an indication of my cat/dog-ness.

Vignette: Harry Truman

Harry Truman, president of the USA at the end of World War II, was known equally for his positional bluntness and his personal humor. The movie *Truman* draws out the difference.[6] Truman clearly saw the difference between himself as a *person* and the *position* he held. There is an ongoing struggle between President Truman and General MacArthurhis military leader in the Pacific. In the passages that follow, you will recognize that MacArthur was a large cat - in fact, he blended his *person* and *position* together. Truman understood that the American President was the commander-in-chief and MacArthur was one of his generals. Truman didn't want to set a precedent that a general was more important than the Office of the President.

Truman once said, "I am just a man holding this office. If I dirty it, it will be dirty after I am gone."

Another time, Truman has warned General MacArthur to stop holding press conferences that interfered with foreign policy. The president hears of the General's last press release and is upset. In essence, he says,

"If he wants to bad mouth Harry Truman he will have plenty of company, but he will not bad mouth the presidency."

1-7

In my opinion, *West Wing* is currently the best TV series to portray the conflicts between *position* and *person* in a group dynamics setting. I recommend that readers watch some of the reruns. In each episode, inevitably one or more characters encounters internal conflicts between what the character *personally* believes in and what is *positionally* (that is, politically) called for.

To explain the relationship between "person" and "position," we will borrow the "x" and "y" axes from mathematics and rename them "person" and "position." The location of "+" and "-" have been altered for our purposes. The "+" indicates a high degree of person or position; the "-" symbolizes a low degree.

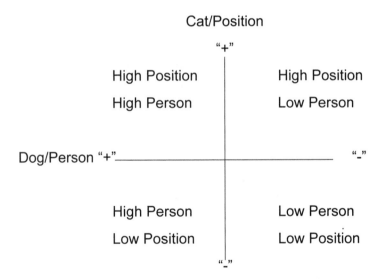

Cat/Position

"+"

High Position
High Person

High Position
Low Person

Dog/Person "+"————————————————— "-"

High Person
Low Position

Low Person
Low Position

"-"

The chart that follows expands the previous chart by detailing the bottom left and top right quadrants.

Cat/Position

"+"

This quadrant is where people operate from their position and not from their person. Probably known by their authority but people don't know the person. If they have leadership, it is based on consistency.

Dog/Person"+" ———————————————— **"-"**

This quadrant is where people operate from their person and not from their position. They are seen by others as a person and devoid of positional power. If they have leadership, it is based on personal contact. **"-"**

So far, the top right and bottom left quadrants have been our focus. What about the other two quadrants?

Cat/Position

This is where one wants to live. Charismatic leaders are systematically inconsistent. They have solid criteria by which they assess every situation. They know guidelines and know when to make an exception. They blend their person and position.

"+"

Dog/Person"+" ———————————————— **"-"**

When someone lacks person and position, they are considered FALOW. (Follow Another Line Of Work.) They have no leadership ability. They are inconsistent: they lack reliability, dependability **"-"** and predictability.

The four quadrants can be labeled as follows:

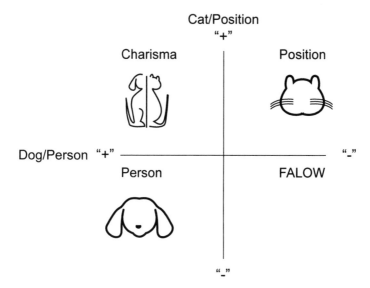

Levels of Responsibility

1-8~9

By adding a diagonal line from the bottom left to the top right quadrants and labeling that line "levels of responsibility," it becomes clear that folks with higher levels of responsibility tend to be more in the top right quadrant (cats) than in the lower left (dogs). The concept of "levels of responsibility" is the variable that influences whether we operate from our *position* or our *person*. The rule of thumb is that the lower the level of responsibility, the more likely it is appropriate to operate from *"person"* and the higher the level of responsibility, the more likely it is appropriate to operate from *"position."*

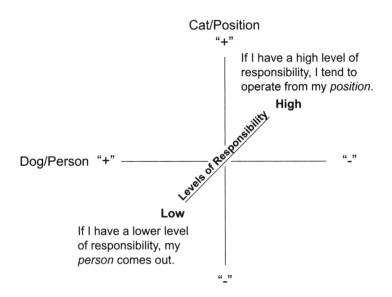

The phrase, "Levels of Responsibilities," warrants clarification. On the surface it seems that a cat, who has high levels of responsibilities, is responsible. The implication is that dogs, with low levels of responsibilities, are less responsible—a gross insult to dogs. Levels of Responsibility and being responsible are not directly connected. A cat can have a very high level of responsibility and not be functioning in a responsible manner. A dog can have a low level of responsibility and be functioning in a very responsible manner. Levels of Responsibility and being responsible are two different concepts.

The bottom half of the "levels of responsibility" line indicates how someone in a lower position operates—high person. The top half of the "levels of responsibility" line indicates the effect of promotion—high position.

The above graphic illustrates the high correlation between an individual's position/job and the individual's degree of dog/cat-ness.

> **The higher the position, the more cats are found.**

Why is this so? Is it because cats are attracted to and promoted to higher positions? Or is it that when someone is placed in a position of high responsibilities, the cat in the individual comes out? Probably, there is truth in both statements. At the lower levels of organization, dogs are the norm. Comparatively speaking, a cat is more comfortable operating from position, while a dog is more comfortable operating from being a person.

A way for me to understand myself is to reflect on how I am in several different contexts. As I think about a committee where I am the chair, my behaviors are more serious and my focus on accomplishment and closure is greater. On another committee where I am just a participant, my actions are looser and more relaxed. This even occurs in my personal life. When it is our turn to have the family over for a holiday meal, my level of tension is higher during the preparation, whereas when we are guests, we approach the event with more levity.

Vignette—A Gender Thing?

Fred usually was the one who was up and showered before Joselyn was out of bed. One morning, as he slowly drifted from his dream state he reminded himself that it was Thanksgiving and he could finally sleep in. He reached over to Joselyn's pillow only to find her absent. He could hear pots and pans being shuffled about in the kitchen. He romantically called out, "Honey, don't you want to come back to bed and 'roll in the hay' awhile?" His amorous invitation was rebuffed. After showering he entered the kitchen with a "Good morning." His cheerful greeting was returned with a perfunctory, "Morning." The awkward silence that followed was broken by Joselyn saying, "The other two families will be here within three hours."

Defensively, Fred retorted with, "I know! I have the suds in the refrigerator and will have the fire going in a minute."

After his second "emergency" trip to the grocery store he noticed that the kitchen had become a command center with the commander-in-chief getting more and more tense. Finally, Fred make the mistake of saying, "Honey, you just don't sound very happy ... let me call them and call the whole thing off. Maybe we can get a restaurant reserva-tion."

Her explosive "NO!" only convinced him that he was right. But her penetrating stare with non-blinking eyes also told him to be still.

While Joselyn was all smiles during the entire din-ner, she emotionally collapsed while cleaning up. Fred chalked up the experience to a "female" thing.

That following summer, Uncle Fred promised his nephew and niece that he and Joselyn would take the kids to Disneyland. It was ten o'clock the night before and Fred was under the car changing the oil and bleeding the brakes. His 45-minute job had evolved past one and a half-hours ... and his bleed-ing knuckle wasn't helping the project. Joselyn opened the door to the garage cheerfully hum-ming. Fred feeling sorry for himself uttered several grunts. Joselyn, remembering the kitchen incident in November, playfully teased, "Honey, you just don't sound very happy ... let me tell the kids that the trip is off."

Fred's first reaction was one of resentment, "How dare she! Look at what I am doing for this family." But the twinkle in Joselyn's eyes led him to rethink his first emotion. He took a deep breath, lay on his back and smiled as it finally dawned on him—it wasn't a "gender thing"—it was a "level of responsibility thing."

As Fred finished up preparing and packing the car he reentered the home with a pledge to help out more around the house. Especially on holidays!

Notes

Chapter Two:
CART

The diagonal line in Chapter One (page 22) can also explain the four descriptors that distinguish a cat from a dog. The four descriptors form the acronym of

2-1~2

C = challenge

A = ambition

R = risk

T = tension

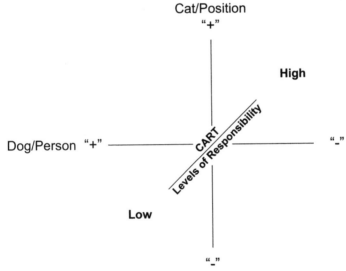

Cats welcome higher levels of **challenge**, have higher levels of **ambition**, and seek higher levels of **risk** and **tension**.

Challenge

2-3

Niagara Falls is home to a legend named William "Red" Hill, Sr. Once a steel barge with three men aboard was being towed by a tug when its tow line broke and it was set adrift. After several attempts were made to throw a line across to the rig, the line became tangled, preventing the buoy from reaching the barge. Red volunteered to swing himself out to the obstruction hand-over-hand above the raging water and untangle the lines. The buoy finally reached the barge and the men aboard were rescued. Red truly loved the challenge of rescuing people from the jaws of nature.[7]

Most people operate within the limited confines of, "We have always done it that way." Cats push the envelope, envision the Panama Canal, discover penicillin and take us to the moon.

Pioneers & Settlers

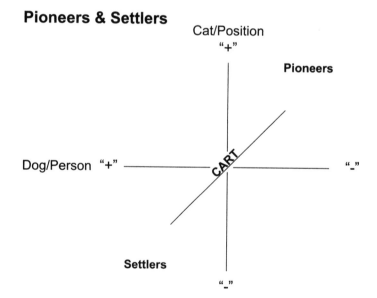

The extreme end of cats are pioneers. They are like the mythical creature, Icarus, who flies so high that the sun melts the wax by which his wings are fastened. To the average person, "pioneers" seem somewhat crazy. The public reads about a CART who dies "in an attempt…" and says, "Fool." When a CART succeeds, our jaws drop open in amazement at the audacity. We still have a part of us that whispers, "Lucky fool." Amelia Earhart and Charles Lindberg are examples. Because Icarus fell to his death, the adjective, Icarian, carries the connotation of too daring, foolhardy, rash.

Lewis and Clark were early 19th century CARTs—they went where "no man had gone before." We hasten to add that pioneers, people who "dream and do," populate both genders—Sacajawea, a Shoshone Indian woman, led Lewis and Clark.

From all accounts, pioneers are "unreasonable" people. "Unreasonable" as in the following quote: "Nothing is ever invented or discovered by reasonable people." For our purposes, we will focus on the pioneer who survives what others call a disaster. How are they? Fine.

> ***Cats land on their feet.***

Peak performers are cats. Watch a professional baseball player take a horrible swing at a pitch. The player immediately steps out of the batter's box and shakes off the memory. Upon finishing a ritual of bodily stretches and clothing adjustments, he steps back in the box with an attitude, "I don't know who did that last swing, but I AM HERE NOW!" A cat's favorite strategy is amnesia—"Let's get on with our next life…we were given nine so we can use all of them… besides, who is keeping track of the count?" The joke is that peak performers are Egyptians because they live in D'Nile.

2-4

2-5

If you would like to practice the "denial" methodology of peak performers, put a Post-it® on your steering wheel. Every day when you safely drive home, look at the Post-it® and review your day.

> *Review in third person.*
> *Program in first person.*

Dogs review their day in first person pronouns—"I really blew it today!" It is a canine guilt trip, self-inflicted and painful. Cats don't experience this guilt. Why not? Because if cats do review their day, they do so in "third person" as in "he did…," "she did…," or a title. For example a cat might refer to his position, "The manager really blew it today!" After laughing at the "manager's mistakes," the cat then shifts to the first person pronoun and confidently looks forward to the next time a similar situation arises, "What I PLAN ON DOING IS…"

Peak performers have amnesia regarding mistakes. So, if you are going to make a mistake, do it as a cat because you will operate more congruently from your cat. Often the mistake isn't perceived by others as a mistake. (See pages 59-62, Numbers 7 and 8.)

If pioneer represents the extreme cat end of CART, what is the extreme dog end of the continuum? Settlers. There are a lot more settlers than pioneers. After Dr. David Livingstone's pioneering work in Africa reached the London newspapers, a group wrote to him asking, "Have you found a good road to where you are? If so, we want to know how to send other men to join you." Livingstone wrote back: "If you have men who will come only if they know there is a good road, I don't want them. I want men who will come if there is no road at all."[8]

Vignette: Dodger & Mac

We live on a busy country road. Eight years ago when we got our kitten, we wished her luck by naming her Dodger. When she is not playing tag with hubcaps, she will slide across the kitchen floor chasing an invisible object. As she bangs against the refrigerator, she immediately regains her composure and licks herself as if to say, "I meant to do that!" In contrast, our dog Mac will wander into a section of our field and inadvertently pick up a blackberry thorn in his paw and come yelping back to the "Ollie, Ollie, oxen free" of our back porch. His facial expression is one of, "I am not certain what I did, but I know I deserve it and I promise not to go there again."

Ambition

In school our "talented and gifted" pupils aren't interested in studying. The teachers, with good intentions, counsel them with, "You have such potential!" By seventh grade, they hate hearing such unmotivating remarks. Like the real cat, they are sleepwalking through life, waiting for something worthy of their attention. Many an innovator didn't do well in school. The concept of cats and dogs explains entire cultures. Industries that have high fluctuation breed cats. The electronic field is one example. The founder of Apple Computers was a drop out.

Dogs are comfortable living with the status quo while cats find freedom in chaos. A dog leader increases efficiency and proficiency by organizing people and systems better. A cat leader lives for a bigger stage on which to perform. There are often three stages a cat goes through. Initially, they are aware of what is the "norm"—which they find distasteful. Next, they will do anything but the norm. This is a random adventure with mixed results. And finally, they figure out what they do want. Not all cats make it to the third level—many linger forever on the floundering level. Cats look at what is around them and ask, "Why?" Only the very ambitious cats ask, "Why not?"

> **"Overreaching is the most admirable of the many American excesses."** [9]

Easily bored, a wealthy cat will jeopardize a fortune for a bigger fortune.

Risk

When one flies into a major airport during busy times, it is common to see other aircraft in the same vicinity. In fact, often two planes land simultaneously on parallel runways. It is common for the passengers to pray that the air traffic controllers are alert, not realizing that these cat-like people are more alert when it is busy.

What we don't realize is that when air traffic is lightest, we are most vulnerable. Air traffic controllers are a special breed. It is a culture of high-risk individuals. They live for the risk.

To explain this phenomenon, picture a real cat. It sleeps over 18 hours a day, yet can spring to complete life in an instant. Often a dog views a cat as lazy, yet from the dead of sleep a cat erupts two feet into the air. That is why some superior athletes don't practice well, yet you want them on your team for the game. There isn't enough at stake during the practice. A cat is most "on" when the risk is the highest. A dog shies from such pressure. Michael Jordon always wants possession of the basketball as the clock winds down. The same is true in ice hockey for Wayne Gretzky; he wants the puck on his stick when time is running out. Michael says he has lost more games than he has won by taking the last shot. Wayne jokingly preaches that you will never miss a shot you don't take. At the end of the athletic contest, dog players pass. Cat players shoot.

> **Dog players pass. Cat players shoot.**

Retired athletes often golf for excitement. It isn't just the golfing, it's the gambling that gets their juices flowing. The game becomes a betting contest, often with considerable financial risks.

Tension

Certain professions attract cats and other professions attract dogs. Artists often have to increase their tension in order to be creative. Gary Larson, creator of the *Far Side*, openly says that he doesn't know where he gets his ideas. And then quickly adds, " I sure hope they keep coming because I have deadlines." Cats have relaxed alertness.

During my high school senior year we huddled together in the locker room before the start of the game that determined if we would advance to the next level of playoffs. The tension was unbelievable. Sensing the anxiety, the coach opened with, "Nervous?" Lots of players nodded vigorously. Then he paused and silently looked everyone in the eye and broke the stillness with, "You should be—it's called excitement!" The team, in unison, laughed in relief knowing their emotions were normal.

Looking back on it now, the dogs nodded their heads when asked "Nervous?" The cats didn't chime in until the coach reframed their feelings as "excitement." The difference between the cat players and the dog players became even more pronounced when coach thoughtfully whispered, "Where would you rather be?" The dogs froze knowing they would rather not have the entire student body counting on them. The cats smiled because they were playing for themselves.

Super athletes are cats who will not give or expect an "inch" from their opponents during a game. And yet, immediately when the contest ends, these same cats exhibit an outpouring of appreciation for their opponents. Only a worthy combatant can take you to your next level of development. Cats respect you if you push them. They hate it if their opponent is hobbled with an injury because they want to know they could beat their opponent at full strength. In the Japanese tradition the ultimate purpose of a martial arts match is to improve oneself. From this perspective the match is a process, not a goal, because "improvement" has no end. The goal of winning the match isn't that relevant; your opponent isn't your enemy, but an ally in your quest to improve yourself.

To counter balance the dogs' view that contestants are "mean" to each other, we offer this story from the unofficial Notre Dame Opponents' Hall of Fame.[10] The Fighting Irish football team approached their last game with a depleted offensive line. The center didn't have any replacement. At the end of the first half, he was seriously injured. The rumor that filtered to the opponent's locker room was that the center had cracked two ribs and was heavily taped up. As the first play of the second half was commencing, the center's opponent asked, "Which side?" The center hesitated to respond because of his vulnerable condition. He decided to trust him and pointed to the injured side. The opponent immediately shifted his position so that he would put pressure only on the center's "healthy side."

Notes

Chapter Three:
Charisma

3-1

As communicators, our ultimate goal is to increase our charisma. We want people to be more receptive to our point of view. How do we get to the charisma quadrant? It depends on where you are on the Levels of Responsibility diagonal line. Two routes to charisma will be offered. As you read them, consider which path is more appropriate for you.

3-2

Cats Becoming Charismatic

If my level of responsibility is high and I am successful in my position, I am most likely operating from my cat. (If my level of responsibility is high and I am not successful in my position, I need to increase my cat.)

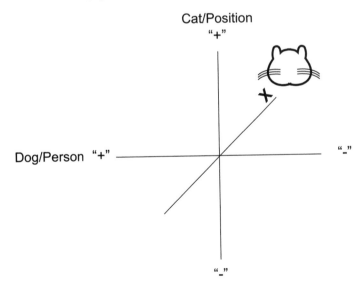

For a cat to achieve charisma, the route is traveled by developing dog qualities.

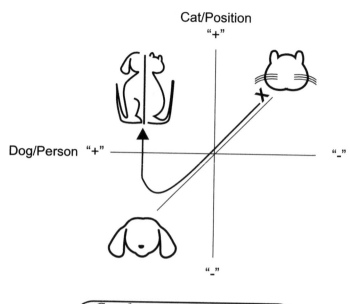

Cat/Position "+"

Dog/Person "+"

"_"

"_"

> *Cats become charismatic by increasing their dog-ability.*

Dog-ability

Dogs want rapport and trust—such traits are often byproducts of the dog feeling known and appreciated. Dogs seek leaders who are genuine, real and authentic. The dogs feel cared for when you do these things:

- Increase personal relationships; know what is important in people's private lives.

  - Listen a lot—be fully present when listening and maintain eye contact.

  - Write down people's birthdays and acknowledge those dates.

  - Learn what is important in their worlds and ask about the latest developments.

- Operate in a more egalitarian manner.

- Become aware of others' contributions and acknowledge them with emotive appreciation.

- Instead of issuing a command, when possible, try to ask for a "favor."

- Be less formal in speech, dress and behaviors.

The behavior that you especially develop is "approachability." One of the easiest ways to understand the importance of employing approachability is to view communication during the decision-making process. The decision-making process consists of the Gathering, Evaluating and Deciding phases.

The Cat Practices Approachability

As a credible voice-oriented individual (males tend to fit this category), your definitive abilities are of high premium during the Evaluating and the Decision phases of the decision-making process. A pilot's voice is an example of a credible voice pattern. Often you have to be careful if you are a subordinate because your voice pattern may cause the superior to be concerned that you are after their job. Once you become a manager, your credible non-verbals are well-suited for positional communication. Even then you have to be careful, because a too-credible voice can cause subordinates to think that they are taking too much of your time and patience. If this happens, the flow of information from those below may not be detailed enough.

If you are a credible-voice superior, make sure you maintain positive relationships with your subordinates by separating the issues of a situation from the people involved. It is acceptable and effective to look at a paper and use a credible, even raised, voice but when looking back at the subordinate, make sure that a soft voice accompanies the eye contact.

To practice the approachable voice pattern:

- When saying words, bob your head up and down rhythmically.

  - At the end of your spoken words, lift your chin slightly to have your intonation curl up.

  - Keep your head up and still until the last syllable's sounds finish. In silence, move your head back to the original position.

You might find it helpful to pretend you are very happy. The low breathing that accompanies smiling produces the approachable effect. Once you have mastered the Pollyanna syndrome, you can modify the sweetness back to a believable version. The other refinements are:

- Stand with your toes not pointed straight ahead.

- Shift position so there is more weight on one foot than on the other.

- Keep your hands in front of your body, with your wrists at the same height as the elbows, so your forearms will be parallel to the ground. Hold your palms up.

- Move your forearms and hands in rhythm with your head. Often your hands look like they are making circles in a rhythmic, repeating manner.

Dogs Becoming Charismatic

3-3

3-4

If my level of responsibility is low and I am successful in my job, I am most likely operating from my dog. (If my level of responsibility is low and I am not successful in my job, I need to increase my dog to seem normal.)

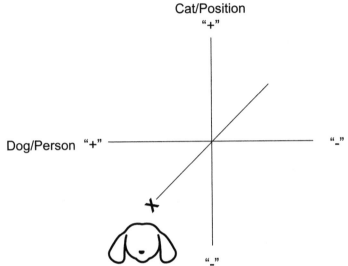

For a dog to achieve charisma, the route is traveled by developing cat qualities.

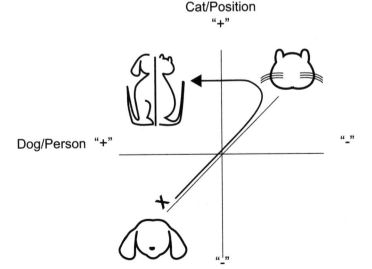

> *Dogs become charismatic by increasing their cat-ability.*

Cat-ability

Cats want productivity and efficiency—such traits are often byproducts of the cat feeling utilized and challenged. Cats seek leaders who are competent, definitive, and willing to buffer them so they can get their job done.

The cats feel empowered and growing when you engage in the following activities.

- Increase working relationships; know the chain of command and ask approval from appropriate parties. (Actually, an extreme cat would "do" and then wait to seek forgiveness.)

  - Obtain the hierarchical chart and a flow chart of the power.

  - Know what the company's values are and refer to them in conversation.

- Become aware of different departments' contributions and factually acknowledge them.

- Seek to be fair:

  - Instead of individualizing each situation, be consistent in managing.

  - Let people know consequences before they are enforced.

  - Value respect over being popular.

- Be more formal in speech, dress and behaviors.

The behavior that you develop is "credibility."[11] (See pages 119-122 and 130-133 for more details.) One of the easiest ways to understand the importance of credibility is to watch how people communicate during the decision-making process. The decision-making process consists of the Gathering, Evaluating and Deciding phases.

The Dog Practices Credibility

If you have more of an approachable voice pattern—and remember that, statistically speaking, there is a higher percentage of females in this category, be aware that your talents often are highly prized during the Gathering stage of the decision-making process. In fact, the approachable-voice individual is often the hub of the wheel that all information is directed to during the initial phase of the decision-making process.

Picture a group of five people at a meeting; four of them have highly *credible* voices and one has a highly *approachable* voice. There is a high correlation between having a *credible* voice and being a power broker. The four individuals are jockeying for the top position in an "I-am-better-than-you" competition. As the meeting progresses, the four individuals often look at the *approachable* individual while actually addressing a response to one of the other four members. The *approachable* individual leans toward the speaking member, asks clarifying questions, and makes sounds while attentively making eye contact. Information is elicited because of the listening ability, facilitation skill, and safety created by the *approachable*-voiced individual.

An individual's innate approachable voice pattern is indispensable during the Gathering of information phase. Yet that person is left out during the Deciding phase.

As the time for evaluating and deciding occurs, no one looks at the *approachable* individual. Confused, the hub is no longer a part of the wheel of power. Suggestion: if you are at the *approachable* end of the voice continuum, make sure you shift your physiology to the *credible* side as the decision-making process shifts away from the Gathering phase toward the Evaluating and Deciding phases. Sit up straight. No smiling. Still body. Flat (businesslike) voice.

> *By shifting to a physiology appropriate for the phase, you remain an influential member.*

To practice the credible voice pattern:

- Hold your head (chin) one to two inches higher than usual.

- At the end of your spoken words, drop your head down.

- Keep your head down and still until you have completed your last syllable.

- During pauses, move your head up so it will be one to two inches higher than its normal position.

Everyone has both voice patterns. The strategy is to recall in what context each was used. Then pretend you are in that context to reaccess the desired voice pattern. Maybe you will find it helpful to pretend you are almost angry. The high breathing of anger or pressure produces the credible effect. Once you have practiced the angry, credible voice, breathe lower before doing the voice. This will give the impression that you are definitive.

The other refinements are:

- Stand with your toes pointed ahead and your weight even on both feet.

- Bend your forearms at the elbows and extend them forward horizontally with palms down.

- Your arms and hands can move slowly while talking. Arms, hands, *and head* should move down in unison at the end of your statement.

Influence and Power

3-5~6

Charisma is when we have love from our dogs and admiration from our cats. Charisma is a blend of our internal cat and dog. A sophisticated way of thinking about this blending is to examine *influence* and *power*. The charismatic individual's first priority is to operate from personal influence, and, if necessary, to be comfortable switching to positional power. The diagonal line (Levels of Responsibility and CART) can also be a continuum for *influence* and *power*. A dog lives by the Golden Rule of, "Treat others the way you want to be treated." A dog hopes that it will influence people through being a role model of concern and caring. A dog says, "Do as I do." Of course a cat humorously describes the Golden Rule as "Whoever has the gold, rules." A cat expects others to follow because of the cat's authority. A cat says, "Do as I say."

3-7

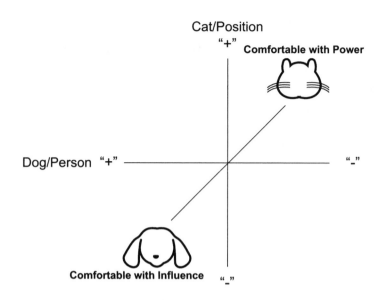

Cat/Position "+" Comfortable with Power
Dog/Person "+" "−"
Comfortable with Influence "−"

3-8

> *It is obvious why a cat, operating from power, can't be charismatic. Passive resistance is always more powerful than active authority.*

Likewise, a dog, operating from influence, can't always be charismatic because there are times when cats won't respect influence. If there is no power to revert to, then my influence is decimated and, at times, destroyed. Often the employment of power is not for the sake of the individual I am managing but for the sake of the group (surely a topic that is vast enough to warrant another book. See Michael Grinder's *Managing Groups—The Fast Track*).

3-9

Fall from Grace

While our goal is to be charismatic, it is equally important to have a recovery plan if we have charisma and fall from grace. Sometimes an incident might occur that initiates the fall from grace. Other times, the seasonal differences between people with higher levels of responsibility and people with lower levels of responsibility trigger a fall from grace. If we have charisma and lose permission, the question is, "In what direction do we retreat: toward the cat quadrant or toward the dog quadrant?"

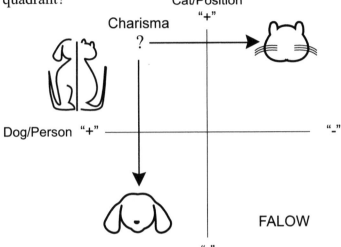

The answer depends on my level of responsibility inside the organization.

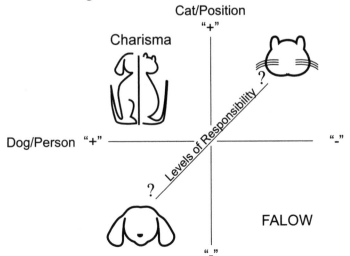

The higher my level of responsibility, the more appropriate it is to move to the cat quadrant. Operating from my cat position will allow those around me to function more fully.

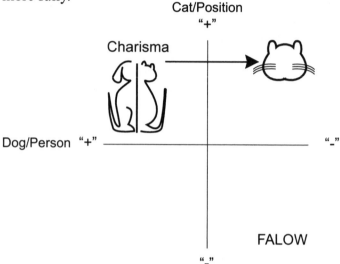

Vignette: Do Your Position

"I sensed early on, however, that the (ROTC) drill team was losing its edge. John was distracted by girlfriend problems. ...I wanted to take the team away from John and give it to somebody else... But John kept saying, 'I can do it.' ...We competed that year...but lost the trick competition... I was angry, mostly, at myself. I had failed the trick drill team, and I had failed John.... too.

"That day, I started absorbing a lesson as valid for a cadet in a musty college drill hall as for a four-star general in the Pentagon. *I learned that being in charge means making decisions, no matter how unpleasant.* (italics added) If it's broke, fix it. When you do, you win the gratitude of the people who have been suffering under the bad situation. I learned in

> a college drill competition that you **cannot** let the mission suffer, or **make the majority pay to spare the feelings of the individual.** (boldness added) Long years afterward, I kept a saying under the glass on my desk at the Pentagon that makes the point succinctly if inelegantly; 'Being responsible sometimes means pissing people off.'"
>
> Colin Powell[12]

The lower my level in the organization, the more appropriate it is to move to the dog quadrant.

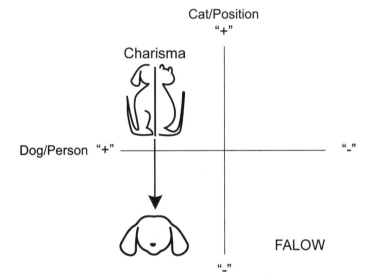

Vignette: Return to Person

Larry Liaison had been with the company for a decade. As an administrative assistant he attached himself to his first boss, Ambitious Abby. His level of competence and sense of loyalty resulted in "coattail promotions." Every time Abby was advanced, Larry was brought along.

In time, the power and prestige of Abby's position was associated with Larry. People knew that the way to get on Abby's busy docket was through Larry. So while Larry didn't have any formal power, his ability to informally influence powerful Abby was widely recognized. Larry was Abby's professional confidant—a safe person for Abby to brainstorm with and to float political balloons with.

It was a gloomy day in winter when Larry received the shocking news that Abby had been fatally injured in a car accident. While union regulations secured his administrative assistant's position to Abby's replacement, Larry was both emotionally and professionally lost. Over time, Larry was comforted by several sessions with a grief counselor. What was most confusing to Larry was the sorting out of his "professional" realm. His normal habit of lingering in his boss's office to further assist the boss's thinking was met with a perfunctory, "Is there anything that isn't clear?"

It took Larry's many subway rides home before it dawned on him that his new boss didn't know him like Abby did. Larry realized he needed to return to his stated job description and wait for the boss to get to know him as a person before seeing if a professional relationship could blossom.

Communication Models

3-10~11

Both the dog and cat believe that *relationship* is the key to success. However, the dog thinks of a personal model whereas the cat thinks of a business model. They define relationship in very different ways.[13]

Personal Model (Dog)	Positional Business Model (Cat)
egalitarian	hierarchical
personal relationships	clear roles and functions
rapport	roles
trust	tasks / clear expectations
friendship	leadership
internal focus	external focus
acts based on feelings	acts based on verifiable data
wants to be liked	wants to be respected
warmth	working together
seeks comfort	seeks fairness / accountability
empathy offered	feedback given
emotional support	professional assistance
ask favors	demand accountability
compromising	clear outcomes held stable
counseling	coaching
assumptions based on interpretations	facts and data
unstructured	structured
psychological considerations	professional considerations

The charismatic leader blends both models. The great Antarctic explorer, Ernest Shackleton, blended the authority of his position with his strength of character to save all his men. The movie, "Master and Commander" with Russell Crowe portrays a similar blend.

When a dog talks about the need for a relationship with employees and subordinates, the dog conjures up images of "rapport" and "closeness," whereas the cat envisions "working" and being "aligned." This chapter forces us to reexamine what is meant by relationship. As students of communication, we understand how the dog seeks personal relationships and the cat professional relationships, yet we want to broaden how to think of the term "relationship." Americans have around 17 kinship terms (mother, father, brother, sister, aunt, uncle, cousin, grandfather...). In contrast, the Arunta, an Australian aboriginal tribe, have several hundred distinctions.[14]

Chapter Four:
Catnip

*"We want to command by our presence
instead of demand by our authority."*[15]

Your goal is to increase your influence with people to
have them be receptive to your vantage point. For most
of us, enticing cats is a more daunting challenge than
stroking dogs. This chapter is designed to help you
intrigue cats.

4-1

Cats are attracted to personal charisma in others. They
also want to figure out how the others have created
their charismatic persona. Don't be fooled by the
shortness of this chapter. This work will equip you
with charismatic leadership tools.

Any competent individual can lead dogs because dogs
are innately cooperative. We need managers who can
exhibit leadership with cats. Although dogs will let you
lead them, cats will not be led. You have to create an atmosphere in which a cat is attracted to fully participate.
An effective manager directs a dog and attracts a cat.
The trick is to get the cat to want to join.

> *A charismatic leader fosters a followship of dogs
> and a fellowship of cats.*

The cat is attracted to high quality things and people.
From a non-verbal standpoint there are eight ingredients of charismatic leadership.

4-2~6

1. Both Cats and Dogs Need Paws

The pause (paws) is the single most essential non-verbal component of communication. One of the positive by-products of pausing is that you and the listener(s) lower your metabolism. When you pause in speaking and in movement, you are seen as intelligent. This maintains or increases the listeners' attentiveness. When you pause, the perception is that you are confident and competent. As a result, you are seen as a charismatic leader.

> *In no way are dogs less intelligent than cats,*
> *nor are cats more stressed than dogs,*
> *and yet that is others' perception of them.*

Whether you are seen as a credible-cat or an approachable-dog, you will increase your value in the group by learning to pause. By p-a-u-s-i-n-g, the cat seems more relaxed and comfortable; this is an ingredient that is needed for a cat because cats often seem to others as too intense or pushy. By p-a-u-s-i-n-g, the dog seems more intelligent; this is an ingredient that is needed for the dog to be valued more because dogs often seem to lack confidence or competence.

4-7~10

2. Frozen Hand Gesture

If you don't pause, it may be because you are concerned that pausing will result in losing the listener's attention. Often a speaker, who is worried about the listener interrupting, will inadvertently make the situation worse by talking with a lot of hand movement. Continuous movement results in the listener not being able to create a picture of what the speaker is saying. However, when you pause with a frozen hand gesture (that is, hold your hand still), the listener has time to stabilize the picture. Simply, use gestures while talking but be still during the pause so you don't mess up their pictures.

3. High Expectations[16]

4-11

When you are not talking, what should you do with your hands? When the hands are akimbo (hands on hips and elbows bent outward) or folded across the chest, other people perceive the person as operating from an authoritarian posture: an angry cat. Likewise, when the person has their hands behind their back or in front in a fig leaf fashion, the person non-verbally conveys that they are pleading for acceptance: a desperate dog.

In contrast, you will increase your leadership by having both forearms at your side, or both forearms parallel to the ground, or a combination of one forearm at your side and the other forearm parallel to the ground. These three postures each communicate, "I believe you are self-reliant and capable," which is one of the goals of every person-in-charge. The positioning of the hands is referred to as "high expectations" because of the results achieved.

4. Breathe through the Nose

4-12

You will be seen as even more intelligent when your lips are closed during the pause. Ideally, the speaker holds her breath during the initial part of the pause. Inhale through your nose, while keeping your head and hands still. When a person moves during the inhalation, the hands and head move back to increase the lung capacity. This is often interpreted as an invitation for the listener to talk.

Breathing through the nose vs. breathing though the mouth explains some cross-cultural prejudices. In Western European cultures, a closed mouth is seen as more intelligent than an open mouth. Think of people sleeping on an airplane—one passenger has their mouth open and another doesn't. Which one looks more intelligent? It is common in third world countries for people to pause with their mouth open. Westerners watching TV footage of third world citizens speaking mistakenly interpret them as being less intelligent than themselves. Understanding non-verbal communication is a necessary step toward removing cross-cultural prejudice.

4-13~14

5. To Join or Not to Join[17]

Catnip opened with *pausing*. The pause is the basis for all eight ingredients of charisma, including "To Join or Not to Join." How the pause is used determines if the content that is said both before and after the pause are joined or not joined. When the pause is used poorly, the listener's brain becomes overloaded, forgetting the information presented; when this happens, the listener will often withdraw from us, seeing us as negative. In contrast, when the pause is used effectively, the listener understands, retains our information, and associates us with positive energy. To use the pause effectively, first decide whether or not you want the listener's mind to join the content that comes before and after the pause.

Join—to Retain Info

If you join the content after the pause with the content

before the pause, the listener only has one bit of information to understand instead of two. The listener pays better attention and remembers longer what they heard. Do the *Join* process when the two pieces of content are related. You connect the two pieces of content by simultaneously *speaking* and *moving* at the end of the pause.

Brain research explains why the *Join* process works. It has been suggested[18] that the brain can handle between five and nine bits of new information. Each time a presenter inadvertently separates chunks of information through the "move and then speak" maneuver, the audience quickly loads up their five to nine slots of information. However, if the presenter "joins" (pauses and breathes) chunks, the listener stacks several bits of information on one of their five to nine slots. The key thing to remember in joining is this: after the pause, do not move a muscle until there are words coming out of your mouth. To be safe, start talking a nano-second before you move. For example, a presenter might open a program and pause after each of the following sentences:

4-15

> "Thank you for coming." (Pause)
>
> "Our purpose is to preview the upcoming quarter." (Pause)
>
> "We will look at three projections. (Pause)
>
> > A. Marketing (Pause)
> >
> > B. Sales (Pause)
> >
> > C. Cash flow" (Pause)

This opening may or may not work well—it depends on the presenter's timing and skill in joining related bits of information. If after each bit of information the presenter moves and then speaks (that is, "separates"), the listeners start getting overloaded. However, by joining the different statements (talking while moving), the presenter makes it possible for the listeners to stack all bits of content in the same slot. When a presenter hooks together related bits of information this way, the listeners will still have mental space slots left for more content.

Not to Join—to Separate Info

If the content before the pause is negative, there is a danger that the negative content might contaminate what you say after the pause. You don't want the listener to be distracted by the negative or even worse, to associate you with the bad news; also, you don't want to dilute the power of the message that follows the pause. To avoid this, you separate the negative content before the pause from the neutral or positive content after the pause. After you have said the negative part, pause and remain silent. Then without a sound, shift your position, and settle into the new position; only then do you start talking again. The *Not to Join* process allows you to "not get shot" as a messenger.

4-16~18

6. Voice Patterns and Breathing[19]

Listeners feel safe when you seem confident and in control. This is a result of your breathing deeply. There are two voice patterns and two breathing patterns. It is the combination of these patterns that provides the safety that the listeners seek. The *approachable* voice pattern is produced when you bob your head while talking; it results in a rhythmic, lilting voice. The approachable voice pattern ends with an intonation that curls up.

The listeners interpret that you are seeking information/input. The *credible* voice pattern is produced when you hold your head still so that the voice pattern is flat and the intonation curls down. The impression is that you are sending information.

If you breathe high/shallow when speaking in either voice pattern, the listeners aren't safe. With the approachable voice pattern and shallow breathing, you run the risk as being perceived as pleading and lacking confidence; with the credible voice pattern and shallow breathing, you run the risk of being perceived as being angry and impulsive. When you breathe from low in the abdomen, your listeners hear the approachable voice pattern as being open to dialogue and the credible voice pattern as being definitive.

7. Recovery

Since we don't live in a perfect world, life is a series of adjustments. In fact, the corporate template of the past was to "PLAN A LOT (e.g., research a need, develop a product / service, investigate via focus groups) and then finally DO (release the goods on the market place)." This template resulted in caution and conservatism. The goal was to be perfect the first time. Companies sought people who were reliable, predictable and accountable.

4-19

Harvard's famed pundit, Roger Fisher (with Alan Sharp)[20] boldly suggests that the exact opposite strategy is now more effective: PLAN A LITTLE, DO, THEN REVIEW. Literally, a company wants to make small mistakes before its competitors. This leads to hiring people who are innovative, risk-takers, and able to operate outside the box. Successful modern life can be summarized by:

> **Recovery is more important than perfection.**

This saying is true if for no other reason than you get to practice *recovery* more often than *perfection*. How does the concept of recovery tie-in with cats and dogs?

> **Part of recovering is accessing the cat in you.**

The cat will continue as if nothing happened, whereas when the dog makes a mistake, the dog is embarrassed and has to apologize. Gregory Bateson, an anthropologist, offers an interesting view of mistakes.[21] When a person is learning a new behavior the person is often unsure whether the behavior will produce the desired effect. If the person's concern that they are making a mistake is evident to the other party, the other party may well be responding to the person's incongruity and not the new behavior. To truly test out a new behavior the person has to be as congruent as possible; that is, they must have their non-verbal and verbal aligned. Employing Bateson's insight, the cat is much more capable than the dog of testing new behaviors.

> *"I've never made a mistake.*
> *I've only learned from experience."*
> **Thomas Edison**

8. Congruency

The Western world puts a premium on eye-to-eye contact. The belief is that when bad news is being delivered, eye contact indicates *honesty*. Let's see if that belief bears out in reality. The messenger of the bad news may honestly think that the news is warranted/justified/appropriate. However, the messenger may also feel bad that the circumstances had to be like they are. This would especially be true if the bearer of the negative news isn't comfortable with conflict. When the messenger delivers the bad news with eye contact, the receiver sees both emotions on the messenger's face: "Yes the news is appropriate," and also, "I feel bad about delivering the news."

If the news is volatile and the recipient is upset with the news, the recipient's emotional reaction will limit the recipient's ability to cleanly sort out the messenger's ambivalence. Also the messenger's own emotions might heighten the recipient's emotions.

When people are interviewed, they usually say that they value eye-to-eye contact. Yet in reality, most of the time people aren't aware whether the messenger delivered the news with or without eye contact. In fact, there are advantages to the messenger putting the bad news on a paper. When the skillful messenger delivers the news, the messenger will look at the paper. By directing the recipient's attention to the paper, the messenger keeps his own emotions out of the situation. The advantage is that when a recipient is unencumbered by the messenger's emotions, he can focus on his own reactions.

What about those times when someone demands eye contact? Yes, some cats will push for eyeball-to-eyeball deliverance. What is called for is "congruency." Congruency is the ability to deliver bad news without a trace of ambivalence. Congruency has the following ingredients:

- Make eye contact.

- Do not blink. Keep your eyes open.

- Use short phrases or sentences.

- Pause often and longer than normal.

- Keep your hand gesture frozen during the pause (your hand moves only when speaker talks again).

- Breathe abdominally during pauses.

- Hold your body still, especially your head.

- Use a whispery voice.

A ready source of congruency is movies. Watch the same scene several times. Use the second hand of a watch and note the length of time between blinks. The length is unhuman. The actors have to memorize their lines so they can focus on how to deliver them. This principle of "knowing our content to emphasize process" is true for us also. To be congruent, we have to have our verbal content memorized.

Regarding the axiom "Recovery is more important than perfection," Dale Carnegie said, "The successful person will profit from their mistakes and try again in a different way."

Chapter Five:
Bonding—Reading a Person

"Advanced technology is
indistinguishable from magic."
Arthur C. Clark[22]

Having mastered the technique for becoming congruent, your next step is learning how to form relationships—especially with cats. One way of bonding with cat people is to intrigue them by "reading" them.

Forming a Relationship with a Dog

5-1

Everyone knows how to develop a relationship with a dog—just give the dog attention. Pretend that the letter "d" in dog stands for direct. A manager who wants to form a relationship with a dog directly approaches the dog and spends time. This includes:

- Being in front of the person

- Leaning towards the person

- Having soft, empathetic eye contact

- Listening by making encouraging sounds

- Saying the person's name and asking questions

- Nodding the head

Of course, while doing these things, one must be genuine and really care. The rapport and trust that come from the direct approach with dogs can be immediate and long lasting.

> *We form a relationship with a dog by satisfying the dog. The dog is happy to have us lead them.*

5-2~3

Forming a Relationship with a Cat

Comparatively speaking, it is easier to form relationships with dogs than with cats. Sometimes the difficult person that we work with is the linchpin to our success we need this person. We don't need a *personal* relationship but we do need a *working* relationship with this cat. You can't go directly up to a cat and say, 'I want to have a relationship with you!" You do it in a roundabout way indirectly. That is, we entice a cat to form a bond with us by teasing it. This chapter suggests that a sophisticated way of accomplishing this bonding is to give the cat person information about them that causes them to wonder, "How do you know that?" We tease the cat by telling it something that the cat thought was hidden from the public that intrigues the cat.[23] The process of getting this information by *reading* a cat is explained in this chapter.

> *We form a relationship with a cat by enticing the cat. The cat chooses to let us lead them.*

The method of forming personal relationships with dogs directly, and forming working relationships with cats indirectly is an alternative to power management. Persistent power management results in dogs passively resisting and cats actively resisting the boss.

Modified Johari Window

The easiest way to explain how to read a person is to look at a model for understanding interactions that was created by two psychologists, Joseph Luft and Harry Ingham.[24] Combining their first names, they called it the "Johari Window." This is a modified Johari Window.

The Cat Person

Myself	What we both know about the cat person	What I know about the cat that he doesn't consciously know about himself
	What the cat knows about himself that I don't know	What neither of us knows about the cat

When teasing a cat, two questions arise: what category of information impresses the cat, and how do I go about obtaining such information?

Tease the cat person by sharing information that the cat knows about himself, yet he wonders how we know such information. The cat is intrigued. The cat person is even more impressed when we *tease* with information that he hadn't thought about before, yet upon hearing the information, he intuitively knows it makes sense.

> *We form working relationships with dogs by satisfying them and with cats by teasing them.*

When I share external physical data that I have noticed such as height and weight, that isn't impressive un- less one is a county fair barker guessing a customer's weight. Cats are intrigued by other people knowing about their personality: their style of thinking, what their tendencies are, how they fit into group dynamics, what motivates them, and their stress tendencies. Even more poignant to cats is accurate feedback about their values and beliefs.

Chart of Cat and Dog Traits

It is important for the practitioner who *reads people* to have enough experience to appreciate when an indicator of a personality trait is accurate and when it might not be. The best method to increase the accuracy of reading a cat is to look for correlations—how many other indicators reinforce the *read*? Otherwise we fall prey to the temptation of reading a person based on only one trait/indicator. Even Freud cautioned his students when he said, "Sometimes a cigar is just a cigar."

The page reference is found next to or below the title of the category. The horizontal line separates the two chapters. Each of the categories is explained in Chapters Six and Seven Tales from the Kennel. Chapter Six emphasizes your internal traits how you are with yourself. Chapter Seven focuses on traits you display when interacting with others. Often these sets of internal and external traits will overlap.

Chart of Cat and Dog Traits

Category	Cat	Dog
Confidence/competency (p. 84)	more confident than competency warrants	more competent than confident
Voice pattern (p. 86)	credible	approachable
Innate traits (p. 87)	ambitious just being themselves	vulnerable very aware of others
People Emphasis (p. 89)	held accountable issues	highly accepting morale/relationship
Gestures (p. 91) Level of influence	palms down greater influence	palms up lesser influence
Self image (p. 95) Perfection	self selects; from internal is motivated by progress	dependent on how others see loves doing the same activity that satisfied others over and over
Purpose in life (p. 99) New things	to dabble and tinker if selects it, is very excited	to be happy wants to do things well
Intrigue vs. Clarity (p. 101)	loves intrigue	loves clarity
Learning levels (p. 102)	drawn to and inspired by complex skills	polish old skills and master new skills
Operates (p. 108)	from their position as the pilot	from their person as the flight attendant
Aware of others (p. 110)	not very aware of dogs	much more aware of cats
Power (p. 113) Seeks	comfortable with it promotion / challenge	shies from it comfort
Conflict (p. 114)	doesn't back away often unaware if they cause the conflict	frightened and confused by it offended if they have to point out something
Average trait (p. 116)	wants to be respected	wants to be liked
Extreme trait (p. 117) When stressed When calm	is arrogant/martinet seen as angry seen as definitive	is guilt-ridden /sycophant seen as pleading / victim seen as seeking information
Management style (p. 119)	intervene early	intervene much later
As parents (p. 124)	assures their children that they are someone	encourages their children that they can be someone
Apology (p. 128)	What are you talking about!	will initiate even when not at fault
Decision-making process (p. 130)	loves to decide	would rather only gather info

5-4

Additional Benefits

The primary purpose of the Chart of Cat and Dog Traits is to increase our ability to *read* a cat. The purpose of reading the cat is to *tease* the cat to seek a relationship with us. By changing the Johari Window from a description of the knowledge between *myself and a cat* to *myself and any another person*, some additional benefits are gained.[25]

The Other Person

Myself	What we both know about the other person	What I know about the other person that he doesn't consciously know about himself
	What the other person knows about himself that I don't know	What neither of us knows about the other person

Because the dog-oriented person finds comfort in clarity, it is impolite to tease a dog. The dog wants *safe* things. Therefore, dialogue with the dog about common knowledge (that is, top left quadrant) "Now you are from San Diego...." In time your permission will allow you to progress to the left bottom quadrant, "What do you especially like about...?" The left quadrants are a gold mine with a dog. The dog feels a closeness because of the attention we give.

Likewise, once we have established a relationship with a cat by teasing via the top right quadrant, we can enter the bottom right quadrant via open-ended questions.

Relationships with a dog and cat are developed by starting with the top boxes and progressing south.

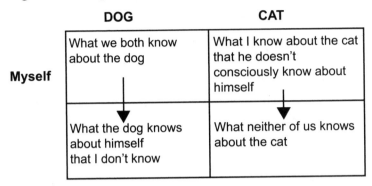

	DOG	CAT
Myself	What we both know about the dog	What I know about the cat that he doesn't consciously know about himself
	What the dog knows about himself that I don't know	What neither of us knows about the cat

Strategy of Reading a Person

The more a person has traits from just the cat column or just the dog column of the Chart of Cat and Dog Traits, the more likely the other traits of that column apply. In essence, an observer can employ the Johari Window in the following manner. Let's say that in four categories of the chart, a person exhibits obvious traits from only the cat column. Since these traits are common knowledge, the cat person won't be impressed with our input—they wouldn't be teased enough. However, because all four traits are from the cat column, the correlations are high and therefore we can guesstimate that the other categories are also true. Since these other traits are not common knowledge, the cat person is impressed by our input. The cat receiving such information wonders what other insights we have to offer.

5-5

The Cat Person

	Known Traits	Less Obvious Traits
Myself	✓ ~~ ~~ ~~ ~~ ~~ ~~ ~~ ✓ ~~ ~~ ~~ ~~ ~~ ~~ ~~ ✓ ~~ ~~ ~~ ~~ ~~ ~~ ~~ ✓ ~~ ~~ ~~ ~~ ~~ ~~ ~~	✓ ~~ ~~ ~~ ~~ ~~ ~~ ~~ ✓ ~~ ~~ ~~ ~~ ~~ ~~ ~~ ✓ ~~ ~~ ~~ ~~ ~~ ~~ ~~ ✓ ~~ ~~ ~~ ~~ ~~ ~~ ~~ ✓ ~~ ~~ ~~ ~~ ~~ ~~ ~~

People—especially cats—are fascinated by themselves. Cats want to be unique and yet are *known* by us—that is an intriguing mystery to them.

> *We read a cat person by silently noticing their known cat traits, and then mentioning the traits that are less obvious.*

Exercise: There will be occasions where we categorize an individual as a cat but then when we share the "read" (that is, the less obvious traits), the individual disagrees with a given trait. When that happens, mentally return to the three cautions listed in the Introduction: Context, Expectations, Comparisons. Here are some questions that will help us be more accurate with our read.

Are we pigeonholing too much? Does the individual have *aspects* of both a cat and a dog? Were we too absolute? In what context(s) was the "read" accurate and in what context(s) was the "read" inaccurate? Context examples might be found in:

- the individual's personal life vs. professional life;

- with people the individual knows compared to being with unfamiliar people;

- when the individual is operating from his *position* vs. *person*;

- when the individual has *authority* and *time* vs. when the individual doesn't have *authority* and *time*;

- when the individual is *gathering* information vs. *deciding* what to do with the information.

Be a good scientist and give yourself permission to ask questions. Learning involves being a good sport with yourself. As previously mentioned, Wayne Gretzky, the greatest ice hockey player of all time, paraphrased risk-taking this way: "You can't make the shot you never take."

Every summer at our little town's annual "Harvest Days Weekend," my adult daughter and I have volunteered at the Food Bank booth.[26] We set up a table with a crystal ball and wear swami hats. Then we practice *reading* people. Everyone knew it was a spoof and yet participants keep bringing their friends to the booth because of the accuracy of the *read*. Whenever Krista and I are off, we ask how we could have been more accurate. Of course, the cat-people are more than happy to correct us—it is great learning.

5-6

Sometimes when we read an individual, the person will assign values to the cat and dog traits. The majority of readers will view the dog descriptors as more favorable than the cat descriptors. In the author's opinion, this is a correct presumption because the majority of people tend to be more dog than cat. When we field tested this manuscript, many readers didn't know why people would want to *really be a cat*. However, one cat friend's reaction was, "So what's your point!" To him, the differences in the descriptions were obvious; he certainly didn't find the cat descriptions troublesome or "de-dogatory."

Assigning values to traits is so prevalent that many job interviews include the questions, "What assets do you bring to this job?" and "What might people at your last job say are your liabilities?"

5-7

When we think about ourselves, we want to be more sophisticated than the job interviewer. Instead of thinking in terms of "assets" and "liabilities," it is more accurate and beneficial to see our innate cat and dog traits as tendencies. Sometimes the traits are assets and sometimes those same traits are liabilities. Charismatic people figure out in which contexts, circumstances, and situations they can be themselves and in which ones they want to be flexible enough to behave in newly-learned ways.

> *I influence others by either being myself or changing myself.*

5-8

Calibrating

Charisma has provided you with a range of cat and dog behaviors that you can select from. You are flexible; you might be more dog with one person and more cat with another person. In fact, you might be more dog with one person in a certain situation and be more cat with that same person in another situation. How do you know which set of behavior is appropriate and effective? You know by understanding how to calibrate the other person's every-changing behaviors.

A human will shift from their *person* to their *position* and from their *position* to their *person* during the same conversation. The questions that arise are: "What are the indicators that such a shift is occurring?" and "What are the appropriate responses?" "How would a manager know if the superior he is communicating with is operating from her person or position?" In general, the more the superior is employing her friendly voice,[27] the more she is operating from her *person*. The more her voice pattern is businesslike,[28] the more she is communicating from her *position*. The manager's skill in accurately interpreting is based on his ability to recognize what the superior normally sounds like. Once the superior's baseline voice pattern is known, then an increase in approachability characteristics indicates her *person* is surfacing. When features of the credible voice pattern appear, then she is switching to becoming more *positional*.

Statistically, the lower the business unit of the organization the superior administrates, the more her baseline voice pattern is approachable. At the higher end of the organization, the superior's normal voice pattern is more credible. Female superiors, because of cultural expectations and anatomical reasons, generally tend to have an approachable voice pattern; male superiors have a cultural and anatomical propensity to talk with the guttural voice of credibility. The superior's gender needs to be taken into account when calibrating their baseline behavior.

Besides voice patterns indicating whether the superior is operating from her *person* or *position*, there are body language indicators. The kinesthetic equivalents of the voice patterns are:

Body Language	Credibility	Approachability
Body	sitting very straight	leaning forward
Head	on top of shoulders	forward and tilted
Listening	head still silent	head bobs makes sounds
Wrist	straight	bent
Weight	evenly distributed	body slanted; more weight on one leg

In essence, if the body is straight, a person looks more credible. When the body is bent, tilted or slanted, a person looks more approachable. The reason that credibility is associated with the superior operating from her position is that characteristics of credibility can non-verbally convey that the information is being sent one way; it is not open for negotiation. On the other hand, approachability is the equivalent of the superior non-verbally sending the message, "I am seeking your input," which is a two-way dialogue approach.

Responding with Flexibility

We have established that there is a general pattern as to who uses the credible and approachable voices. Lower level employees and females statistically have an approachable voice pattern; higher level business managers and men have a credible voice pattern. There are exceptions to these patterns and the distinctions between these two patterns can be subtle. However, based on these patterns, we want to be aware of the following dynamics:

5-9

- In speaking with an approachable voice, lower level business units/female superiors are inviting the subordinate to person-to-person. This superior is expecting the subordinate to respond in an approachable voice pattern.

> **Vignette: Quarterly Reports**
>
> Richard, punctual as always, gaveled the regional managers' meeting to order at exactly 9:00 a.m. Business had been great. Many of their satellite offices had been elevated to being staffed with full time managers. The hiring and training of these

new office managers had been the company's last quarter's focus.

Regional manager Pat reported first. "Our two new managers are doing very well. Both offices had high functioning employees so we placed two female managers there. Forgive the stereotypes female managers are statistically better listeners than male managers. We wanted to make sure we didn't disturb the productive atmosphere."

- In speaking with a credible voice, higher level business units/male superiors are fostering the subordinate to operate on the issue level of communication. If the subordinate responds in a credible voice, his boss will give more credence to what the subordinate is saying.

Vignette: Quarterly Reports (continued)

Janet, followed Pat with, "We had three satellite sites that were upgraded successfully. As a side note, Sally, our top consultant, has mentored one of our perennial weaker sites. Sally found that the manager was credible oriented and the manager wasn't listening to the employees' suggestions. She determined that the manager was competent but not flexible. She taught the employees to sit up straighter and use a credible voice pattern when making suggestions. We are optimistic the site will increase in productivity."

- When the superior increases her approachable voice pattern and the subordinate doesn't match her by also using an approachable voice pattern, the superior is *personally* hurt.

> **Vignette: Quarterly Reports (continued)**
>
> Frank trailed Janet with, "We may need Sally to visit our region. We didn't open any satellite offices, but we have closely monitored one of our veteran sites. The Culver Town center has blossomed with Mrs. Limber in charge. We moved her from the valley office; she wasn't doing well there, and yet we felt she had good management skills. It seemed that the valley store wanted an "all business" manager— which wasn't a good fit for her personal style. The Culver employees are more complex—they want to do their work but also want high morale. Mrs. Limber can show both her "person" and her "position."

- When the superior increases her credible voice pattern, thus indicating her positional power, she will expect the subordinate to operate from the approachable voice pattern because the superior interprets such behavior as submissive. When the subordinate doesn't comply, the superior perceives that her position is not being honored.

Two vs. Three-Point Communication

While the above is what the superior expects, *Charisma* suggests the subordinate use a more flexible approach. Instead of memorizing the four axioms above, remember to do the following. When the subordinate is looking at the superior, it is referred to as two-point communication because there are two parties involved. When making eye contact, or two-point communication, it is recommended the subordinate be more approachable. When the subordinate looks at the piece of paper, the communication is known as three-point because there are three entities: two humans and the piece of paper. When the content is volatile, the communicator displays

the information visually. The paper serves as a third
point. When both the subordinate and the superior are
looking at the piece of paper (the third point), the subordinate has the option of being credible. By avoiding
eye contact and focusing on the paper, his business-like
voice will add credibility to his ideas without offending
the boss.

5-10

Linguistic-Neuro—A Menu of Choices

Your ability to make effective decisions is based on the
quality of the information you gather. When you don't
have permission to openly seek information, you can
use a backup strategy called Linguistic Neuro. Instead
of asking questions, you say several statements, each
with different possibilities. In essence, you offer a menu
of choices. As the statements are said, you watch the
reaction of the superior. The strategy is so named because you are using language/words (linguistic) and are
observing the other person's "neurological" response.

Linguistic Neuro can be useful in many situations. For
example, sometimes the cat is a superior and is not sup-
posed to share information that they are privy to, and
yet you need to know it in order to be an effective negotiator. If you directly ask and the superior says, "Sorry, I
cannot share that with you!" a gap between you and the
cat is created. By reading body language, you learn the
information without the superior having violating these
covenants.

Examples of Linguistic Neuro include evidence of a
person's reaction such as a shift in facial expression
(visual indicators), voice pattern (auditory indicators),
posture (kinesthetic indicators) and breathing. If the cat

stiffens, the cat is showing a negative reaction, and if the cat relaxes, the cat is showing a positive response. In essence, the cat doesn't have to say anything because the cat's non-verbals are speaking. Because of the sophisticated nature of calibrating what the cat looks like normally and what the cat looks like when the cat has a silent non-verbal reaction to what you are saying, it is recommended that you see a demonstration of this skill and practice it under the supervision of a trainer/mentor. For more training information, visit www.michaelgrinder. com.

After you mention each of the options, pause (with a frozen hand gesture). The reason for the pause is to separate the cat's neurological response to each of the options. If you don't pause, you run the risk of mistaking the cat's reaction to the previous option for the current one.

You can use Linguistic Neuro to gather information in many different situations—the list is endless. Some examples include:

- *Time:* "It is possible that the meeting could be as soon as today (pause), **or** within a couple of days (pause), **or** the next time you have an opening in your schedule."

- *Pressure of Power:* "You would know best if this decision is something that can be made entirely at our building (pause), **or** if the district office needs to be involved (pause), **or** if input from the home office is appropriate."

- *Information:* "In going forward, there is the question of information: do we have all the information needed (pause), **or** do we have most of it (pause), **or** is some necessary information not available yet?"

- *Procedural:* "We could call a meeting (pause), **or** send out a memo (pause), **or** contact each person individually."

- *Value/Needs:* "There are several possibilities as to why the distributor's reaction during last week's conference was so disturbing: it could be that we felt distrusted (pause), **or** betrayed because we have done so much for the distributor's company (pause), **or** not respected for our view point."

Once you have a sense of the information you are seeking, you may want to verify your impression. For example:

- *Time:* if the superior's face (visual indicator) softens (positive reaction) when you mention "…an opening in your schedule," then, as a negotiator, you could say, "Well, why don't we meet the next time you have a window of opportunity?"

- *Value/Needs:* if the superior shifts her body (kinesthetic indicator) into a more tight posture (negative response) when you say, "…betrayed …after all we have done…" you can say, "While we may feel the distributor is an ingrate, we may still want to..."

In the first example, you are seeking a positive response and you then direct the course of action. In the second, you seek a negative response and want to acknowledge the superior's emotional reaction, because once the superior's person is acknowledged, her needs are met and then she can be more rational.

Vignette: One More Time

Jannella rehearsed the night before with her friend Ismal how Jannella would broach a sensitive topic with her boss. "Now Ismal, I have been talking to you about my role as the event coordinator for some time. I want you to pretend to be my boss and not want to share information with me. Just guess what he might say."

Ismal, "You want me to 'breast my cards'?"

Jannella, "What does that mean?"

Ismal, "It is an expression in Bridge (cards) where you hold your cards close to your chest so that others can't see them."

Jannella, "Perfect." She straightens her back, glances one last time at her notes and begins,

"Mr. Crabtree, our conference is two months away and the more advance information we have, the better we can orchestrate the conference's success. When will we know the number of participants who will be attending?"

Ismal, "We won't know until the last minute, so plan for between 100 to 120 participants."

Jannella, "Now the most important information deals with the support materials. We could have the presenters submit handouts that we can reproduce in packet format. [long pause]

"Or we could request that the presenters submit their PowerPoints and indicate which slides they want the group to take notes on. We would then run off three slides per page, with lines to the right for note taking. [long pause]

"Or we could just provide the usual LCD projector

for the presenter and blank note pads at the participants' round tables." [long pause]

"Ismal, that was my dry run. I wanted to practice
the wording. Now let's do it one more time. This
time I will practice watching your reactions to the
choices. There are three choices: handouts, print-
out of important slides, or notepads. This time pick
one of the three choices as your favorite, one you
dislike and the third choice you are neutral about."

Exercise: With a partner, practice Linguistic-Neuro.
Give the person three choices. After a dry run of practicing the wording, do it again and this time have your
partner like one of the choices, dislike one choice and
be neutral about the third. If you don't have a partner,
rehearse in your mind; think of someone in your real
world with whom you want to do this strategy.

Linguistic Neuro is one of the best ways to "manage
upwards."[29] It is as if you, as a negotiator, have a crystal
ball and can see into the cat's person. In actual truth,
you are respectfully seeking information without violating the superior's position. The quality of the possibilities (linguistic) you list will determine the quality
of neurological responses you see. If you observe no
change in the other person's response, it is safe to add a
"none of the above." For example:

5-11

- *Information:* After you say, "In going forward there
  is the question of information. Do we have all the
  information needed (pause), **or** do we have most
  (pause), **or** is some of the needed information not
  available yet?" If there is no shift, you may want to
  add, "**Or** we may not have asked the right questions
  yet."

- *Procedural:* You could add, "We could call a meeting (pause), **or** send out a memo (pause), **or** contact each person individually." "Or perhaps a combination of these (pause), or perhaps an approach we haven't mentioned yet."

Chapter Six:
Tales from the Kennel—
You with Yourself

*A good story is remembered twice: once when it is
read, and again when it is reflected upon.*

Many of us remember a concept better when it is associated with a story.*

Chapter Six has the stories for the top half of the Chart
of Cat and Dog Traits (page 67). The stories are about
our internal cat and dog traits. Chapter Seven has the
stories for the bottom half of the Chart. It focuses on the
external cat and dog traits.

As you are entertained, allow yourself to drift from
reading the page to reflecting on yourself and other
individuals who are represented by the characters in the
vignettes. Seek to understand yourself and others in a
non-judgmental way.

Each trait is explained in detail along with a vignette
to illustrate the trait. When the character's name in the
vignette begins with a "D," the person is portrayed as
a dog. Likewise, a name beginning with the letter "C"
indicates a cat.

---

*In the index under "Vignettes," the vignettes are listed by title.

6-1

Category	Cat	Dog
Confidence/ competency	more confident than competency warrants	more competent than confident

The cat is ambitious and seeks promotion. Because the cat lives on higher rungs of the corporate ladder than the dog, the cat is used to being unpopular. Being "liked" is all-important for the dog but not for the cat. The replacement for the Peter Principle[30] is,

6-2

> *Don't get promoted past your level of catness.*

A cat presumes it can do anything and therefore struts around with an air of complete and utter confidence. A dog who acted like that would be violating its unwritten pledge to humility. Dogs have to be reassured that they are doing a job to the boss' satisfaction. Since cats invented independence—they operate as if there are no bosses; therefore, the only one a cat has to please is itself. In summary, a dog will have more competency than the confidence to believe and act on its confidence. A cat won't know if it has more confidence than competency until it is in a position where the competency is called for. The cat isn't bothered by discovering he isn't as competent as he thought he was.

> *The cat operates on the axiom,*
> *"Why not go out on a limb?*
> *Isn't that where the fruit is?"*[31]

Vignette: Vying for Promotion

Darla and Carla have each been with the company for five years. They have similar backgrounds with identical degrees. A week ago, Darla had heard that an opening was about to be listed. Away from work, she reflected with friends that she thought she could do the job. Intellectually, Darla knows she is most capable but needed to have others emotionally reassure her. Darla awaited the listing; she was ready, or at least she thought she was.

Carla didn't even know that an opening was in the offing. As both entered the lunch room Darla was a step in front of Carla. There posted on the employment board was the job that both were qualified for. Darla's eyes lit up as she quickly scanned the description to make sure it was within her competency reach—it was. As Darla and Carla started to remove the lids of their Tupperware containers, Darla squealed to Carla, "Did you see the posting?"

Carla, "What posting?"

Darla excitedly points to the bulletin board. Carla causally waltzed over and after barely reading the description matter-of-factly says, "Great."

After, what was an awkward silence for Darla, she hesitantly spoke, "So are you interested in the position?" Darla, always aiming to please, hadn't considered that she might be competing against someone she knew, which would create a sticky situation for Darla.

Carla's response shocked her even more, "Oh no! I am not interested in THAT position, but it will be a stepping stone to where I want to go eventually."

Darla sat in silence, shocked and bewildered by the unexpected turn of events.

Finally by Tuesday, Darla had settled herself down enough to broach with Carla why she hadn't been herself for a couple of days. She vulnerably poured out her reaction to competing with a friend. She was thankful that Carla was slower and more gentle than normal. Carla shared that she operated from a different perspective than Darla. In fact, she shared Diane Sawyer's quote,

"Competition is easier to accept if you realize it is not an act of aggression or abrasion. I've worked with my best friends in direct competition. Whatever you want in life, other people are going to want, too. Believe in yourself enough to accept the idea that you have an equal right to it."[32]

6-3

Category	Cat	Dog
Voice pattern	credible	approachable

There is a connection between an individual's position and their voice pattern. The higher the position, the more likely the individual has a flat voice pattern that curls down at the end of phrases and sentences. This form of speaking is known as being "credible." In *Credibility*,[33] Kouzes and Posner state, "Credibility is the foundation of leadership." It is odd to hear an individual in a lower position speaking in a credible voice pattern. In fact, sometimes a cat needs to be promoted before his voice pattern sounds normal.

Vignette: The Floors

Clarice and Darin started as mailroom employees at the same time. Their superior explained that, "In this organization you really do start at the bottom." It took them a full year before they ever left the doldrums of sorting the parcels in the windowless basement. In their second year, they began delivering to the various offices in the nine-story building. They noticed how upper management had the best views. Because their favorite British TV comedy was "Upstairs, Downstairs," they nicknamed the top three floors as "upstairs" and the bottom three levels as "downstairs." To complete the list of monikers, the middle floors were referred to as "brackish."

They were particularly giddy on the day they received their two-year pins. Over lunch they reflected on their experiences. Darin said how much he enjoyed distributing to the downstairs because the people always say "Thank you." Clarice countered with "Oh no, the upstairs is much more interesting because I make it a contest to see if I can get anyone to even acknowledge me."

Category	Cat	Dog
Innate trait	ambitious; just being themselves	vulnerable; very aware of others

6-4

The letters in *cat* stand for **c**apable, **a**mbitious and **t**alented—at least that's what the cat thinks. The letters in *dog* represent **d**ocile, **o**ther-directed and **g**roup-oriented. The "o" also signifies **o**bedience. Cats presume that others are honored to serve them. Dogs never assume; they are vulnerable and seek to please others. Dogs are team players. A cat is a team of one—the rest are ancillary. At our seminar on *Charisma—The Art of Relationships*, the presenter instructed the participants to form groups of three to engage in a certain role-play. To assist them to form the triads, she suggested that they hold up fingers to indicate they need another member. Of course, most people who were short a third were holding up two fingers and hawking, "Have two, need one." They were doing this while moving around the room. However, a c-a-t was standing in the corner, not moving, holding up one finger and jokingly said, "Have one, will accept two lucky people."

Vignette: We've Struck Oil

Carl and Donald are vice presidents of a medium-size oil company. CEO Barbara values each of them for the assets they bring to the corporate table. Carl pushes and drives the company and its people to new heights. He is often oblivious to the effects of his style. Barbara gave him a toy steamroller for his performance review. In contrast, Donald is the father confessor. His door is not only "always open," he even listens after hours. Barbara often describes him as the morale doctor.

Barbara conducts the weekly meetings by looking at Carl to know if the agenda is moving fast enough and glancing at Donald to determine if the group dynamics are functioning well enough. Like the gauges on a fine oiled machine, Donald and Carl are the yin and yang of the company's health.

6-5

Category	Cat	Dog
People Emphasis	held accountable issues	highly accepted morale / relationship

Cats see people as a means to an end. Subordinates are held accountable in a fair and equitable manner. The group is more important than the individual member. Dogs operate in exactly the opposite way—the individual is to be honored at all costs.

In this regard, the differences between cats and dogs can be overlaid on Fisher and Ury's model of the levels of communication.[34] Their template has the following levels:

Relationship
Motives/Needs
Issues

Cats focus on the issue level and have to be taught to be attentive to the people involved (relationship). Dogs, drawn to people, have to be coached to expand their focus to include the issues involved.

	Relationship	Dogs start here and have to work down.
	Motives/Needs	
Cats start here and have to work up.	Issues	

Actually both models are templates that are appropriate for certain contexts. The military, out of necessity, functions from the premise that the good of the whole outweighs the needs of the few. Gandhi also operated from this premise. The world of counselors is exactly the opposite. The unit (e.g., family) can only function when each individual member is healthy.

Vignette: Synthesizing

Periodically, Carl storms into Barbara's office yelling to her (and anyone else who will listen), demanding that so-and-so be fired. Barbara rotates between a strategy of allowing him to vent like Mount St. Helens, and demanding that he walk around the block before they talk further.

If, after settling down through venting or walking, it sounds like Carl has a legitimate complaint, Barbara will ask Donald to join them. Donald is a humanitarian—an original "chicken soup." He believes that most people can be molded into capable employees. Donald historically will argue that the start-up time it takes to inculcate a new person into the company outweighs the financial and human cost of mentoring a deficient worker. Traditionally, Carl counters with an equally valid premise that we can't fly like eagles if we are surrounded by buzzards.

Barbara describes their arguments as Carl being the thesis and Donald the antithesis. Barbara's purpose of meeting is to arrive at a synthesis.

Category	Cat	Dog
Gestures	palms down	palms up
Level of influence	greater influence	lesser influence

6-6

6-7

People are quite systematic about their behaviors. What people communicate with their eyes is also reflected in their voice, body (including gestures), and breathing. In fact, to the layperson, the term *congruent* means the individual's words are supported by their non-verbals.

When a person has a flat, credible voice pattern, the person usually has their palms facing down. The direction of the palms keeps the voice flat; likewise, the palms facing up support an approachable voice pattern. It might be wise to note that in many Western European cultures, a woman speaking with her palms sideways (that is, facing each other) is the equivalent of a male communicating with his palms down.

Some cultures believe in "majority rule," which works if everyone has equal ability to persuade. Dogs operate on the axiom that if they are nice to others then others will be nice to them. This familiar *Golden Rule* is accurate among dogs. However, it is not an accurate representation of cats or *mixed (animal) company*. If a committee of ten has two cats, six dogs and two *dot*s (people who are mostly *dog*s but have some *cat*), the two cats will dominate disproportionately to their numbers. This is because a cat's non-verbals are more powerful than the non-verbals of other members. The following exercise illustrates this.

Exercise: To illustrate that cats dominate (this is an extension of "Voice Patterns of Domination" on page 86), role play the following exercise. Three people are seated. One chair is facing two superiors of equal status. The solo chair is proposing the details of a company party—such details as location, food, activities, games, speakers, and invitees. One of the superiors is credible (back straight, head still, silent, and looking at watch every 20 seconds). The other superior is approachable (leans forward, bobs head, makes encouraging sounds, makes eye contact).

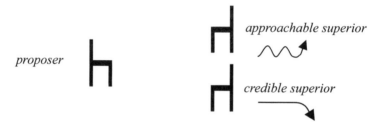

After doing this role play for two to four minutes, read the following patterns of domination.

1. The proposer looks at the approachable individual during the *Gathering* phase of the decision-making process longer and more often than at the credible individual. The proposer is breathing better when making eye contact with the approachable listener.

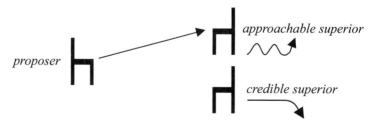

2. When the proposer looks at the credible individual, the proposer increases her stress as evidenced by the proposer having difficulty finding words.

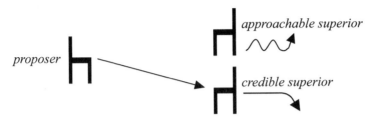

3. The exception to number one and two correlation is a proposer who is innately power-oriented. The more the proposer is credible, then the less the proposer makes eye contact with the approachable individual. In fact, the proposer is dismissive of the approachable individual because the proposer seeks alignment with the power-based individual.

4. At the end of the *Gathering* phase of the process, proposers will look to the credible-oriented listener as the *Evaluating* and *Deciding* phases are entered. Once the *Gathering* phase is complete, the approachable individual is left out of the process.

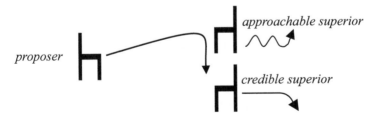

When the proposer says the sentence, "So what do you think?" he switches his glance away from the *approachable superior* and looks directly at the *credible superior.*

It behooves *approachable people* to recognize when the decision-making process is nearing the end of the

Gathering phase so they can start switching to the non-verbal behaviors of the *credible voice pattern*. By doing this, the *approachable person* will be more fully appreciated by the other members during the Evaluating and Deciding phases.

Likewise, it is prudent for the *credible people* to increase their non-verbal behaviors that are associated with *approachability* during the Gathering phase so that they can obtain more information.

The previous exercise may help explain why hierarchical organizations keep *credible people* around. Although the *credible people* may be detrimental during the Gathering phase, they shine when the group process gets to the Deciding phase.

In conclusion, effective managers have a full range of voice patterns. They use the approachable style when gathering information and the credible style when deciding.

Vignette: Another Pair of Eyes

Barbara is attending a meeting with a company that her firm has merged with. Barbara bought the company especially for their famed accounting and research and development departments. This morning's meeting is with the senior managers from several departments.

Because Barbara needs to be attentive to the content, she has brought Perceptive Priscilla from Human Resources. Barbara has instructed Priscilla to watch the palms of the managers of the new company. During the morning coffee break, Barbara and Priscilla huddle in the ladies' bathroom to compare perceptions. They concur that the members of the accounting department gesture with their palms down and their voices sound emphatic. In contrast, the research and development managers speak with their palms up, and their voices sound friendly and inviting.

Barbara phones her secretary to arrange afternoon meetings between each company's accounting and R&D department managers. Wisely, Barbara instructs Carl to chair the accounting department's meeting. He is specifically tasked to make sure the new members don't bully or buffalo the veteran members. Meanwhile, Donald is appointed as the facilitator of the R & D department meeting. His duty is to create an atmosphere of acceptance so that the new members will feel safe enough to share the secrets of their successes.

Category	Cat	Dog	
Self image	self selects; from internal	dependent on how others see	6-8
Perfection	is motivated by progress	Loves doing the same activity that satisfied others over and over	6-9

The cat views itself as self-sufficient, a complete island unto itself. A cat decides its own reality. A dog, which seeks being liked, is highly concerned with how others see him.

Regarding the second characteristic above, *perfection*, there is University of Miami research that sheds some light on this discussion.[35] Researchers found that a boss needs to give six compliments for every one mild criticism. *Charisma* offers these additional distinctions. Since most people are more dog than cat, the statistics stand as stated. But that might be because dogs select *praise* over *progress*. True cats are motivated by neither praise nor accomplishment. The "Donald Trumps" of the world are not driven by money; they would *risk* two fortunes for a chance at a third. It is the "hunt" itself that is their impetus.

While a dog might compliment another dog on the courage it took to *risk* —that same compliment falls on deaf ears when offered to a cat. High performers are most alive when living what dogs call a risk. Certain occupational cultures are filled with cats that live for the adrenaline rush. As previously mentioned, air traffic controllers and professional athletes are such breeds. A look at the performing arts reveals how the artists' perfection is obtained. Ballet dancers are a unique blend of relaxed perfection. Dancers spend their career creating what, to the public eye, looks like an ease of movement. The public is awed by the dancers' fluidity and grace. Yet we know that for most people, their bodies would tighten up if they were aware of all the eyes on them. How do the dancers handle the risk? It isn't a risk to them. It is an opportunity to perform what they love. Emotionally, they are not risking.

It has been medically documented that professional racecar drivers increase their adrenaline, but their heart rate doesn't increase. This results in more oxygen to the brain, thus allowing for greater flexibility in responding. In essence, the cat is not risking, but welcoming the opportunity.

These comments on adrenaline allow us to return to the University of Miami research. Since a cat wants to get better and better (they love self-selected, endless challenges), they want six suggestions for every one compliment. The temptation, when doing a performance review with a talented and gifted subordinate, is to give a plethora of compliments. The smarter choice is to offer suggestions that fit the person's self-selected interests.

Vignette: Readying People for Promotion

Barbara gears up for her annual meeting to set company goals. She intentionally mixes performance reviews of her two vice presidents into the session. Barbara realizes that too often she selects Carl or Donald for a given interaction or project based on their inherent strengths. This is all well and good for her as a CEO, yet it doesn't set a good example for the up-and-coming talent in the company.

She wants to increase those behavioral competencies that both Carl and Donald can model for them. Keeping in mind what motivates Carl and Donald [as indicated in brackets] Barbara approaches Donald in the following manner. "Donald, your commitment to the betterment of this company [other directed] is exemplary [appreciation]. I want to ask a favor [accessing the personal relationship] of you. Cathy and Devon have been identified as candidates for promotion. Both are excellent at the level they are currently operating. And yet, for their future positions they both need more varied communication skills [these people, whom you care about, are counting on you for gaining the competencies that they are missing]." Barbara went on to indicate that "When briefing Cathy before a meeting, show her the techniques on paper that you will be using during a meeting. Then look at her and tell her how the techniques will increase productivity because of the increase in relationship. It is impossible to sustain high expectations without high working relationships. With Devon, acknowledge that he doesn't like unpleasant situations and therefore tell him to write or show volatile information on a flipchart."

Turning to Carl, Barbara first makes sure she has his attention and then looks out the window as she speaks [teasing him]. "Carl, you are dangerous to yourself when you don't have a project you can fully immerse yourself in. Your professional lifestyle is like a cat; you seem to be resting but you are always coiled to spring on something that catches your eye and holds your attention [Johari Window with a positive reframe]. There are two projects that we are looking at [cats love choices]. One will be selected and initiated during this quarter. Both of them have the potential to lift this company to the next plateau [progress]. Before we talk about them [the projects are not being talked about yet so that the carrot on the end of the stick can dangle longer—thus increasing the appetite], I want you to pretend you are the CEO. Think about what you would do with this company if the financial resources doubled [the cat's ego is addressed]."

Barbara could peripherally see that Carl's mind had been hooked. She waited in silence for another minute. When she indirectly saw that his lips were about to move, she spun around away from the window and looked directly at him. This interrupted his impulse to speak—he was stunned. With Carl in a rare state of being cognitively vulnerable, Barbara, without blinking, whispered, "You need to find this opportunity w-o-r-t-h-y o-f y-o-u-r c-h-a-l-l-e-n-g-e. You will need to be patient with the length of the projects, supportive of people, and kind to certain competitors." As if on cue, the phone rang; Barbara non-verbally waved them good-bye as she answered the call. Barbara wanted Carl and Donald to increase their own repertoire by helping subordinates get ready for their promotion. She motivated Carl and Donald to help others by calling on each of their values.

Category	Cat	Dog
Purpose in life	to dabble and tinker	to be happy
New things	if selects it, is very excited	wants to do things well

6-10

There are many categories of cats, one of which is the "talented and gifted." This particular cat's school life is one of waiting for some aspect of a semester to catch their fancy. When that happens, they throw themselves into the course; otherwise, they are just marking time. They are the students who comprehend what the teacher is explaining before the other pupils do. What interests them is not what is being said, but the tangential topics. Being "exceptions to the rule" themselves, they are much more drawn to the substructure and extrapolation of what they are exploring. Teachers privately dub them the "what about..." students. No rules or consequences threaten or move them. These are the students who, by seventh grade, are tired of teachers privately telling them, "You have such potential!"

Most classes are made up of dogs—students who flow with the current; cats describe them as "drifting with ...." When dog-like parents are interviewed as to what they want for their children, they collectively report, "For them to be happy!" That is a realistic goal for dog offspring.

Henry Ford, duly proud of his assembly line invention, was once walking through his office with a time efficiency expert. As they passed near an employee who was sound asleep at his desk, the expert mentioned, "And get rid of him."

Henry turned to an executive who was part of the entourage, "Whatever we are paying this expert for the day—do so now. His work is done."

The man, quite shocked, demanded an explanation. Henry's reply indicates his own appreciation of cats, "The last time the man woke up, he made me a million dollars." The obvious implication was that Mr. Ford didn't want to take the chance of the man sleeping at a competitor's desk.

6-11

Vignette: Cags & Dots

Barbara knows that descriptions of people as cats and dogs are commentaries on the extreme ends of the animal continuum. Most people are in between the two poles, with more people clustered towards the dog end. To identify a person's tendencies, she has mentally created what she calls *dots*. The *"do"* are the first two letters of *dog* and the last letter "t" is from the last letter in *cat*. In other words, the person is 2/3 dog and 1/3 cat. People who have the reverse mixture are termed *cags*. Over the years Barbara has come to realize that to some extent she attempts to surround the cats in her organization with cags which are somewhat surrounded by *dots*.

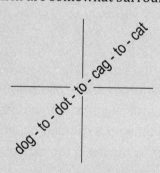

Barbara once explained that engineers need drafters (she used to called them "draftsmen" but has been politically corrected). The engineers will initially be enthusiastic about a project, but in time they become bored. Their strength is in imagining and creating. They fondly cite Einstein, "We have to have more time to imagine." In contrast, drafters see their lot in life as being steadfast; they rate high on persistence.

In Barbara's lexicon, engineers are *cags* and drafters are *dots*. From the CEO standpoint, someone has to finish the projects who can still communicate with the originators.

Category	Cat	Dog
Intrigue vs. Clarity	loves intrigue	loves clarity

6-12

Because dogs want to be happy, they seek clarity. Because cats like being intrigued, they have a higher tolerance for ambiguity. In the military, oftentimes an outcome is funneled down without the method for achieving it. To dogs, this is mentally complex and emotionally perplexing. The cats feel honored that they are trusted to figure out the creative "means" on their own.

A common strategy in hypnosis is the confusion technique. The conscious mind is like the dog part of all of us—it wants to understand. The conscious mind will focus on something that doesn't make sense, at least for a while. Then something else appears that demands our focus and we drop the previous focus. The unconscious mind never quits ruminating; it is like the operating system of a computer that keeps running in the background and never stops. The unconscious mind wants to make sense and will continue to grapple with that which is not clear and integrated. This explains why we can be driving a car (the conscious mind) and, "out of the blue," a thought pops up that relates to something that occurred two hours to two weeks ago (the unconscious mind).

Vignette: Brainstorming Guidelines

Barbara has definite guidelines regarding brainstorming. Invite cats to attend. Why? Because cats will entertain absurd thinking longer, whereas dogs want to take each idea and linearly figure out how the concept would be implemented. Of course, working with cats isn't all upside. Because cats are credible and judgmental, the task of the facilitator in a brainstorming session is to prevent the cats from arguing the merits of ideas.

Barbara's second guideline for brainstorming is to take breaks for distraction. This includes physical walks, food, social activities (favorites: charades, Balderdash™, Hilarium™, Password™, Catch Phrase™). She doesn't always have permission, but when people are receptive, she encourages meditation and power naps.

Barbara has a third rule for brainstorming: involve dogs in brainstorming just before holidays. Normally, dogs are convergent thinkers—they seek closure. During certain seasons, like just before a holiday, the dogs increase their creative thinking capacity and act more like cats. They become more divergent thinkers.

6-13

Category	Cat	Dog
Learning levels	drawn to and inspired by complex skills	polish old skills and master new skills

Adult learning in a training room can be viewed with four levels of learning. Dogs like the first two levels and cats the last level. Ambitious dogs and patient cats are drawn to the third level.

1. Polishing: Reminding the participants of what they already know. It is the equivalent of Stephen Covey's skill of "keeping the sword sharp." (*7 Habits of Highly Effective People*)

2. Mastering: Learning a new skill, practicing it in the training room and actually being able to do the skill.

3. Introducing: Practicing a skill that will need to be practiced further outside the training room in order to be mastered.

4. Inspiring: Demonstrating a set of complex strategies that is currently beyond the participants' ability to practice but within their perceptual grasp. This is a level where the instructor shows what is humanly possible.

Dog participants are drawn to the first and second levels of learning and have to be encouraged to work their way towards the third and fourth levels. Cats, who like to be teased, are intrigued with the fourth level of learning and have to be reminded that they will eventually obtain such abilities by being attentive to the second and third levels of learning.

Vignette: Flexibility

Barbara's favorite seminar leader is Michelle. Michelle offers all four levels of training. Barbara and Michelle design trainings based on the number of dogs or cats that will be attending, which is often determined by which departments are attending. When Michelle has "mixed company," she literally puts the advanced level skills on flipcharts on the side wall of the training room. If the room is mostly dogs, she spends more time in the front. When the key cats' attention begins to wane, she glides over to the sidewall and zaps the audience with a sophisticated extrapolation of the current, simpler skills that she is teaching from the front of the room. After a while the sidewall becomes the Mecca for the cats. In fact, sometimes she merely steps towards the side wall and while looking at it, muses aloud, "You may be wondering how this, what looks like a simple skill, will be the foundation for a more advanced strategy..."

If the room is filled with cats, Michelle opens the program by showing off some sophisticated maneuvers. One time, she worked with the sales force. Successful salespeople have the external clothing of a dog. Barbara refers to these gregarious stars as "people who have never met a stranger." Yet, looks can be deceiving; internally, these successful salespeople are self-sufficient cats. They have to be in order to handle the *rejections* that come with cold calls. Knowing that the stars would need to be teased, Michelle asked for three volunteers whom she had never met before. They came up to the front of the room. Michelle proceeded to describe each member's values, beliefs, and style of thinking. She told them when their assets were present, and what to watch for when they are stressed. Of course, she did this based on the *Chart of Cat and Dog Traits* you are presently reading. Once Michelle's audience knew she had something they did not have—something they wanted, she could proceed.

The maneuver was a gigantic tease because the program wasn't about reading people, but about paper work—the bane of people-oriented stars. She explained that filling out the "Client Informa-

tion Sheet" helps them record important information about their client. She reminded them of how
it feels when Barbara not only sends each of them
birthday cards but appreciation cards on the an-
niversary of when they started with the company.
She ended the day with this teasing quote, "You are
too good not to be better."

Chapter Six Reflections: Many of the vignettes center
around Carl the cat and Donald the dog. They are the
vice presidents of a medium-sized oil company. Barbara, the balancer, is the CEO. As readers, we can identify
with many of the situations that are portrayed. Several
concepts and their emblematic vignettes are worthy of
our second look:

- Of those people I am in charge of, how well do I
  balance them like Barbara does?

- What has Barbara modeled for me that I can
  use? How can I draw out the best in both my
  cats and dogs?

- Regarding the Golden Rule (page 91), being
  nice to a cat in anticipation of the cat being nice
  in return is as logical as the matador telling the
  bull he is a vegetarian.[36] In what situations do I
  need to operate outside the Golden Rule?

- Consensus is a decision-making model based
  on everyone having equal ability to persuade
  others. Knowing that a cat's non-verbals are
  more imposing than a dog's non-verbals. How
  do I quiet the cats so the dogs feel safe enough
  to speak?

- The concept of the proposer (page 92) shows how one's influence is connected with phases of the decision-making process. How will I remember to shift my position when the group changes to the next phase of the decision-making process?

- How well can I recognize my dog and cat tendencies?

- How well can I recognize and accommodate dog and cat tendencies in others?

- The concept of self image (page 95) is key to expanding my range of professional behavior.

  - In what context(s) does my self image allow me to expand my behavior?

  - In what context(s) does my self image get in the way of my growth? How could I suspend my self image so that I can grow in this context(s)?

The idea of "Cags and Dots" (page 100) expands the cat and dog concept:

- Where would I place myself on the full cat-cag-dot-dog continuum?

- Which kinds of people do I function best with?

Chapter Seven:
Tales from the Kennel—
You with Others

A person discovers himself through others.

This Chapter expands the bottom half of the Chart of Cat and Dog Traits on page 67. The emphasis is on understanding our external cat and dog parts. Allow yourself to drift from reading the page to reflecting on your interactions with people. Someone once said that being surprised is the hardest situation to handle. These explanations and vignettes provide insights that reduce or even eliminate " bad surprises."

Many of us remember a concept better when it is associated with a story. In the index under "Vignettes," the vignettes are listed by titles.

Each trait is explained in detail along with a vignette to illustrate the trait. When the character's name in the vignette begins with a "D," the person is portrayed as a dog. Likewise, a name beginning with the letter "C" indicates a cat.

7-1

Category	Cat	Dog
Operates	from their position as the pilot	from their person as the flight attendant

An individual has a part of himself that is his "person" and another part that is his "position." Examples of these differences abound. There is an expression in the military, "Permission to speak freely, sir!" that indicates the subordinate is asking his superior if he can offer a subjective (personal) opinion.

In a court of law, the equivalent is, "Permission to approach the bench?" The trial attorney is requesting an opportunity to communicate not from her public position, but to clarify from a more personal perspective. Of course, the judge can also initiate the confab by demanding that the attorneys report to "chambers." This often is a longer and a more severe form of shifting from public positional postures to a more behind-the-scenes conversation (or reprimand). It is generally acknowledged that trial lawyers are a special breed. It is common for a lawyer to be roundly put in his place by a judge. If the lawyer is operating from his *person*, he could be devastated. However, if he is operating in the capacity of an attorney, then it was his position that was humbled. Colin Powell advises, "Avoid having your ego so close to your position that when your position falls, your ego goes with it."[37]

Vignette: The Flight Home

That weekend Darla boarded a plane for her bi-yearly trek to her mom's. As the aircraft crept towards the runway, she was still preoccupied with her own reluctance to apply for the position. Then suddenly, as if awakened from a dream, she became acutely aware of something she had experienced a dozen times but had never heard—the voice patterns of the pilot compared to the flight attendant.

First, the captain came on indicating the altitude and length of the flight. His voice was measured, guttural with an intonation that curled down, and accented with frequent pauses. Darla realized that such a voice conveys confidence.

Next the flight attendant announced the service that would be offered. His voice was rhythmic, had fewer pauses than the pilot, and had an intonation that curled up at the end of each sentence. Darla recognized the non-verbals of the approachable voice pattern; it carried warmth and friendliness.

Initially, Darla was confused by her new awareness. She gradually sorted out that as a passenger her number one priority is a competent pilot, whereas she expects the flight attendants to be accommodating. The epiphany was that the pilot's credible voice conveys confidence, while the flight attendant's voice conveys a desire to be accommodating.

That night on her mother's shoulder, Darla had a good cry as she shared her day and proclaimed, "I am just a flight attendant!" Tenderly, her mother whispered, "Do you *want* to be a pilot?"

7-2~3

Category	Cat	Dog
Aware of others	Not very aware of dogs	Much more aware of cats

In any public group, the members who have the most credible voices tend to dominate; conversely, those members with the most approachable voices tend to be the least dominant.

Exercise: Without indicating when dominating is appropriate, do the following exercise and notice the listeners' reactions. Pair up with someone and have one person use only the credible voice and have the other party use only the approachable voice. Since our interest is in the "process" of the voice patterns regardless of the content, have the subject be the weather. Talk for two minutes. Then have the parties switch the voice patterns. The subject this time is that the two of you, on a lark, bought a lottery ticket and won millions of dollars. Dialogue for two minutes on what to do with the money.

The suggestion is that the person who initiates her view first will influence which of the following patterns of dominance occur.

7-4

Voice Patterns of Domination	
Who States Their View First	**= Resulting Pattern of Dominance**
Credible voice	= Approachable voice interviews an expert
Approachable voice	= Credible voice interrogates

When the setting is not a public gathering, the pattern of dominance is not as strong because the members know one another.

There are several correlations that flow from the concept of *Voice Patterns of Domination.*

Credible individuals are not aware of the effect they have on the approachable person. This pattern can be extended to include whole groups of people. For example, Canadians are very aware of the effect their neighbor, the United States, has on them. Since 90% of Canadians live within 100 miles of the American border, the media influence is omnipresent. As a result, the Canadians feel dominated by the U.S. But Americans are, by and large, oblivious to their influence on Canadians and the resultant resentment. The same thing is true of New Zealand and Australia. It is common when one is flying to Australia to fly through the Auckland airport in New Zealand. In the shops one can find T-shirts with such expressions as "I support the NZ Rugby Team and any other sporting team that can beat the Aussies." Comparatively speaking, the Aussies are unaware of the Kiwis' burning desire not to be *second chair* to their neighbors.

The synonyms for a credible-oriented person are: positional, leader (assumes permission) and "cat." The synonyms for the approachable-oriented person are: personable, pacer (builds permission) and "dog."

Vignette: Increasing Flexibility

While Barbara truly appreciates all that Carl and Donald mean to her company, she wants the next "Carls" and "Donalds" to be more well-rounded. Having spotted Cathy and Devon as the "future," Barbara arranges for them to take a road trip with her. The Boston negotiations are an ideal training ground for them. Upon arriving, Barbara and entourage attend the perfunctory dinner with the other company's negotiators. When the social hour is finished and just before dinner is to be served, under pretense of a conference call, Barbara huddles with Cathy and Devon in the hallway. Barbara asks them to hold up their index fingers. "Now I am going to ask you a series of questions. After each question I will count to three and you either point to yourself or to the other person to answer the question. First question: Which of you asks the most social/personal questions? One, two, three." Without hesitation, both pointed to Devon.

"Second question: Which of you inquires the most about their company? One, two, three." Both immediately pointed to Cathy.

"Third question: Which of you did they look at when they asked questions about our company?" Based on Cathy and Devon having one eyebrow higher than the other, Barbara knew they weren't readily arriving at an answer so she counted slowly, "O-n-e, t-w-o, t-h-r-e-e." They both slowly pointed to Cathy.

"So we all agree that you, Devon, have great rapport skills and you, Cathy, are seen as the credible one. Here is your task. During dinner, swap functions. By the end of the meal, have the people see you, Devon, as the credible one and you, Cathy, as the approachable one."

Category	Cat	Dog
Power	comfortable with it	shies from it
Seeks	promotion/challenge	comfort

7-5

In the dairy industry, the cream rises to the top. In the corporate world, cats are "cream." While a dog might fret about having power over people, a cat welcomes the power. From the cat's perspective, she has superior *cat*pacities—of course she wouldn't hesitate to qualify herself as someone who knows what is best for other people. The bigger the cat, the more power she seeks.

The cat views competition very differently than does the dog. By knowing how the cats look at contests, the dogs might have a more gentle interpretation of competition. Because the cat is motivated by improvement, the score is a way of measuring the improvement. The contest is not an end in and of itself. The contest is a process of refining one's abilities. Of course, most cats want to win and yet the ambitious cats don't see their opponent as their enemy. The opposition is the cat's ally in their quest to improve.

Vignette: The Next Level

Carroll and Daryl grew up together sharing a common love for playing all sports. Their deep passion was basketball. After each played some college ball, Daryl settled in as a CPA while Carroll ran a staffing company. By the time their children were in fourth grade, they both were coaching their kids' teams. Their desires to be around the game led them to become referees. Eventually, they moved up to handling high school games. In time, they established themselves as an accurate and fair tandem that could skillfully manage a game.

As they rode together to the district meet in another town, they shared what each of them had heard—that they were being scouted to move up to the collegiate level. Their reactions to the possible promotion were very different. Carroll, chomping at the bit to operate in such a spotlight arena, wanted to spend the time high-fiving. Daryl was stoically withdrawn. Though confused, Carroll recognized the need to tone down his enthusiasm. Slowly, Daryl let down the drawbridge to his heart. He wasn't expecting the pending invitation. Carroll was stunned. He reminded Daryl that for three seasons they had been given identical evaluations. Carroll checked to see if his partner thought he needed more experience to progress to the next plateau. Daryl shyly conceded that he did have the necessary training. It took some talking for Daryl to clarify what was in his craw—he didn't want that level of responsibility.

While it took Daryl some time to figure out his own resistance to being promoted, it took Carroll even longer to sort out his feelings. Initially, Carroll couldn't accept that he was any different than Daryl in ability or ambition. By the next game, Carroll shared his discovery. He had unearthed what was generating his resentment of Daryl's not wanting to progress—he was losing his childhood buddy.

7-6

Category	Cat	Dog
Conflict	doesn't back away; often unaware if they cause the conflict.	frightened and confused by it; offended if they have to point out something.

When dogs growl at each other, they are trying to determine who would win if they did fight. If they do end up fighting, it is because they have had a breakdown in communication. Cats are very different from dogs.

They each believe they are a tiger. Many of us feline owners have experienced our cat getting into a scrap with an alley cat. We faithfully take the cat to the vet and pay the expensive bill. We keep our furry friend in the house for three months to have the wounds heal. And, don't we know it, the first time out of the door the cat goes looking for another fight with his nemesis—resulting in another visit to the animal doctor.

Vignette: At the Vet

Cathy and Doris are doctors at a prestigious veterinary hospital. While there is no question that the entire staff is comprised of highly capable people, they do differ over priorities. Often Cathy lacks *dog*plomacy at the weekly meetings. Both her voice tone and selection of caustic words inflame several members. Doris only offers her opinion if the atmosphere is calm and cooperative.

If assistants are remiss in carrying out functions, Cathy impulsively reprimands them. Cathy is often called on the carpet by the head vet for her lack of timing. Cathy doesn't identify with people on a personal level, but operates on the issue level. When Cathy criticizes her assistants, she expects them to professionalize rather than personalize the feedback.

Doris silently gives the person a second (and often times, third and fourth ...) chance. When the infraction is serious, she asks to see the aide in her office so that privacy can be maintained. Doris spends as much time asking about staffer's children as she does getting around to the reason for the meeting. Often Doris takes the transgression personally and is hurt that the person would do such behavior on her watch.

7-7

Category	Cat	Dog
Average trait	wants to be respected	wants to be liked

Wanting to be *respected* and wanting to be *liked* are fine traits. A balanced person has aspects of both. When a cat, who innately wants *respect*, becomes imbalanced, the desire for respect exhibits itself as *arrogance*. Likewise, when a dog, who naturally seeks being liked, is imbalanced, he blames himself for not "being liked" and feels guilty that he must not be pleasing others enough.

Vignette: Utilizing Strengths

As planned, at the six-month mark of the merger, Barbara is reflecting aloud with Priscilla. Some of the departments are operating extremely well. The old and new members of the R & D team, when given freedom within budgetary guidelines, are progressing well on the new projects. Priscilla reminds Barbara how important it is for her to stop by once a month and acknowledge their continuing contributions. Barbara replies, "I need that reminder to visit with them because then they know they are appreciated."

They both agree that when the veteran accounting department members ask the new members their opinion on something, the integration of the new members becomes more complete. Barbara writes herself a note to coach Carrie, as department head, to do this more often. Barbara openly requests that Priscilla monitor Carl's interaction with the two critical departments. When Carl is emotionally under control, he is viewed by the auditors as decisive, which they like, even when they disagree with him. And yet, when he attends the R&D pow-wows, he can be demanding—which is OK if he doesn't stay on his soapbox too long.

Category	Cat	Dog
Extreme trait	is arrogant/ martinet	is guilt-ridden/ sycophant
When stressed	seen as angry	seen as pleading/ victim
When calm	seen as definitive	seen as seeking information

7-8

7-9

7-10

Under pressure, the arrogant cat will be perceived as impatient and angry, an uncaring individual who thinks only of himself. When stressed, the guilt-ridden dog will be perceived as an emotional doormat, a helpless victim of circumstances who pleads to be liked.

Those of us who are egalitarian will tend to misinterpret people who talk in a credible voice pattern as being upset. Likewise, those of us who are innately hierarchical will tend to misinterpret people with a rhythmic voice pattern as likely being doormats.

Actually, it isn't the voice pattern that causes the misunderstanding, but the accompanying breathing patterns. Understanding the following formulas is essential for an accurate interpretation.[38]

Voice	+ Breathing	= Interpretation
credible	+ high	= anger
credible	+ low	= definitiveness; sending info
approachable	+ high	= pleading
approachable	+ low	= seeking information

These axioms are especially important for organizations. Because the higher positions tend to use credible voice patterns, there is a high likelihood that subordinates will misinterpret what they hear. The superior intends to be definitive, but if he breathes shallow/high, the employees think the boss is in a bad mood. In order to seem definitive rather than angry, the boss must breathe low. Likewise, an employee wants to be seen as cooperative, but if he breathes shallow/high, the superior thinks the employee is whining or pleading. In order to be seen as a person with a backbone who can contribute, the employee must breathe low. The breathing pattern, not the voice pattern, is the determining factor.

There is a scene in *A Few Good Men* where Tom Cruise has Jack Nicholson on the witness stand.[39] Tom intentionally irritates Jack to the point that Nicholson's shouting shows spit coming out of his mouth. Most of us equate shouting with being out of control. Jack Nicholson is the consummate actor—he is breathing deep/low, not shallow/high, when saying, "You can't handle the truth!" The proof that Jack is emotionally in command of his character is how his face completely changes as he is immediately arrested.

I identify more with the approachable end of the voice pattern continuum and therefore have had to learn to employ the credible voice with deep/low breathing. One of the advantages of holding my forearms parallel to the ground, which is what the effective credible voice pattern people do, is that I can monitor my breathing and make sure I am breathing deep/low. Since my hands are held in front of my abdomen, I can physically feel my stomach move as I exhale and inhale. So, while I would rather not shout like Jack Nicholson did, I want to regulate my breathing to be deep/low whenever I am credible, especially when I am talking in a loud voice.

Vignette: When Stressed

When Carl is impatient, he appears arrogant and angry to both departments. The accountants want to take him on, while the R & D people withdraw and feel guilty.

Priscilla pleads with Barbara to keep Donald away from the accountants, "when things get heated Donald wants to be liked and doesn't hold them accountable."

Category	Cat	Dog
Management style	intervene early	intervene much later

7-11

When managing a group, there are times when an individual is other than productive. Because the functionality of the group has to be preserved by the person-in-charge, the person-in-charge has to manage the individual. The wisdom of whether to immediately intervene and manage the individual or to wait and manage the individual later is best determined by understanding the culture of the group.

The more the person-in-charge recognizes their own innate intervention style, the more they can adjust to the present circumstances. When you are basically credible, you'll be fine dealing with a credible-oriented group, but you'll need to increase your patience if you are in charge of a bunch of approachable people.

A credible-oriented person-in-charge can be themselves while dealing with a credible-oriented group but must increase their patience when interacting with an approachable-oriented group. On the other hand, if you are basically approachable, but you are in charge of a group of credible people, you'll need to intervene sooner than you normally would. Although you might be uncomfortable, that early intervention will work well for the group.

Managing an approachable group can be tricky; in this type of culture, whenever the person in charge intervenes to manage someone, the approachable people may say one thing in public—"You were too harsh,"—but privately, they appreciate the intervention.

Below are the four combinations that occur when a person-in-charge manages an inappropriate individual in a group setting. Because of the complexity of group dynamics, a triangle is the icon. This is because pressure felt on one side is equally experienced by the other two sides. The corners are represented by P (person-in-charge), I (individual) and G (the group as a whole).

The flat line with the arrow pointing down at the end symbolizes the credible voice/culture. The rolling line with the arrow pointing up at the end symbolizes the approachable voice/culture.

Credible Culture

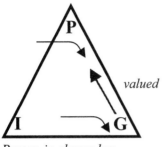

valued

Person-in-charge has excellent timing.

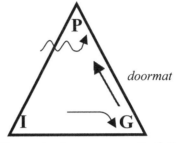

doormat

Person-in-charge seen as "soft;" needs to intervene sooner.

Approachable Culture

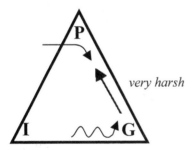

very harsh

The person-in-charge is seen as harsh; needs to be patient. Person-in-charge won't be bothered by the group privately criticizing her.

Credible-oriented people-in-charge need to increase their awareness of the individuals.

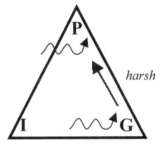

harsh

The person-in-charge is naturally patient, and when she finally intervenes, she is bothered by the group's private criticism of her.

Approachable-oriented people-in-charge need to notice the people as a whole group.

When the group is an approachable culture, the person-in-charge is seen as harsh when managing the individual. The credible cat person-in-charge isn't bothered by the group's reaction, whereas the approachable dog person-in-charge is bothered. The dog often apologizes to the group which confuses the group. It is dangerous to manage from your dog persona. The approachable member privately appreciates that the person-in-charge intervened, but he won't show his appreciation in public. The following research explains this phenomenon.

Friesen and Ekman did an experiment in which they videotaped the facial expressions of American and Japanese people as they watched a horrific film of an industrial accident. Because the Japanese culture places a higher value on masking one's emotions, they expected to see less emotional reaction from the Japanese participants. And, in fact, when an official-looking, white-coated experimenter stayed in the room with each participant as he or she watched the film, that's exactly what the researchers found.

The American participants showed a wide range of distressed facial expressions, while the Japanese participants responded with polite smiles, if at all. Things changed, however, when study participants were left completely alone to watch the film. When they thought nobody was watching them, the people of both cultures showed similarly distressed facial expressions. This led Friesen and Ekman to conclude that even when a culture has strict rules about public displays of emotion, its people still use the same basic facial expressions in private.[40]

Vignette: Stretching

Barbara is always thinking of how to perpetuate not only the company but also the fine tradition of building capacity within the company. Having tagged Cathy as a future leader, Barbara longs to increase her managerial flexibility. Knowing that Cathy's knee-jerk reaction is to step in and control situations, Barbara pairs Cathy with Donald for chairing an upcoming project. The members assembled for the project will be divided into three teams. The individual team's composition is classic. One team is mostly made up of cats, another group has all dogs, and the third a mixture of styles.

Cathy meets biweekly with the three subgroups. Donald, in his role of "behind-the-scenes mentor," has given Cathy the seminal work by Tuckman on the stages of group formation: storming, forming, norming and performing.[41] The cat group quickly enters the storming phase as several members vie for dominance. Donald says nothing as Cathy steps in and lays down the operating ground rules; one tiger in particular has to be put in his place—with Cathy wagging her index finger in his face. Within two weeks, the group was performing well. It was as if Cathy's intervention allowed them to skip to this final level because Cathy's iron hand was the "norming." The only thing that Donald debriefed her on was the length of her display of adamant emotion. Donald, "As soon as the tiger starts to shift from pugilist to cooperation, back off. Learn to give cats a graceful line of retreat."

Cathy's initial impression of the dog group was one of high cooperation. Yet, closer inspection showed that the group didn't have enough drive to push for progress. Cathy's intervention was one of indicating how disappointed she was and she reminded them of the timelines that they were expected to meet. Donald was upset at her vehemence. He explained, "You can demand, as you did, and they will increase their speed of progress; yet, you are handcuffing yourself by having to attend every meeting in order for them to stay on course. Think about how to entice them to depend on themselves so they will perform well even when you are not there."

Having been privy to the brewing storm in the mixed team, Donald advised Cathy not to attend the group's meeting. He explained that in the past the U.S. Forest Service intervened whenever a fire broke out. In 1995, they changed their policy and how to evaluate each fire—and often let certain ones burn. As Donald summarized, "You don't have to fix everything."

7-12

Category	Cat	Dog
As parents	assures their children that they are someone	encourages their children that they can become someone

J.C. Penney was so driven as a parent that he reviewed the ABCs with his child with each of the letters representing a desirable trait A – ambition, B – boldness, C – courage. On a personal note, I am the second oldest of nine children. At family reunions, we often reminisce with "Remember when…" Upon further reflection, it seems that many of us siblings had different moms and dads.

My snapshot of early adolescence and beyond is the move from a modest neighborhood to a fancier neighborhood, one where we were a couple of financial steps below the other families on the street. The new home was the runt of the block. We had four cars so that two would work on Monday morning. My dad was silently present. Since I was more cat-like than dog-like, my father's style was ideal for me. I had tacit support without pressure. He was my best man at my wedding. While I don't recall any encouragement conversations with quiet-dog dad, I do with creative-cat mom. "You do whatever you want... and do it the very best." In later life, her words reverberated like an Army recruitment poster. Taking pride in whatever I did was a recurring theme. My guess is that the socioeconomic differences of our second neighborhood added a chip to the Grinder shoulder; as a result, we all grew up with an independence from outside fashion pressures and rites of passage.

Vignette: Parenting

Driving home from the company's Fourth of July picnic, Barbara laughs to herself when she realizes that while Carl wants his children to assume they are important, he micromanages so much that they can't develop as their own individual selves. Donald, on the other hand, is gentle and supportive of his children. When Barbara met Donald's children, they were self-confident and well-mannered. Barbara was so impressed with Donald's kids that on Monday she asked him if he found parenting easy. He immediately smiled, "Oh, if I only had the first two I would think it was easy. That third one, Carolyn, keeps me humble. I have such a need to be needed—Carolyn operates as if she doesn't need anyone. The farther I am in the background of her landscape, the more useful I am."

When Children Turn Into Cats by Adair Lara[42]

I just realized that while children are dogs, loyal and affectionate, teenagers are cats.

It's so easy to be the owner of a dog. You feed it, train it and boss it around, and it puts its head on your knee and gazes at you as if you were a Rembrandt painting. It follows you around, chews the dust covers off the Great Literature series if you stay too long at the party and bounds inside with enthusiasm when you call it in from the yard.

Then, one day around the age of 13, your adoring little puppy turns into a big old cat. When you call it to come inside, it looks amazed, as if wondering who died and made you emperor.

Instead of dogging your footsteps, it disappears. You won't see it again until it gets hungry, when it pauses on its sprint through the kitchen long enough to turn its nose up at whatever you're serving. When you reach out to ruffle its head, in that old affectionate gesture, it twists away from you, then gives you a blank stare, as if trying to remember where it has seen you before.

It sometime conks out right after breakfast. It might steel itself to the communication necessary to get the back door opened or the car keys handed to it, but even that amount of dependence is disagreeable to it now.

Stunned, more than a little hurt, you have two choices. The first—and the one chosen by many parents—is that you can continue to behave like a dog owner. After all, your heart still swells when you look at your dog, you still want its company, and naturally when you tell it to stop digging up the rose bushes, you still expect it to obey you, pronto. IT PAYS NO attention, now, of course, being a cat. So you toss it onto the back porch, telling it it can stay there and think about things, mister, and it glares at you, not deigning to reply. It wants you to recognize that it has a new nature now, and it must feel independent or it will die.

You, not realizing that the dog is now a cat, think something must be desperately wrong with it. It seems so antisocial, so distant, so sort of depressed. It won't go on family outings.

Since you're the one who raised it, taught it to fetch and stay and sit on command, naturally you assume that whatever is wrong, it is something you did, or left undone. Flooded with guilt and fear, you redouble your efforts to make your pet behave.

Only now, you're dealing with a cat, so everything that worked before now produces exactly the opposite of the desired result. Call it, and it runs away. Tell it to sit, and it jumps on the counter. The more you go toward it, wringing your hands, the more it moves away.

Your second choice is to do the necessary reading and learn to behave like a cat owner. Put a dish of food near the door and let it come to you. If you must issue commands, find out what it wants to do and command it to do it. BUT REMEMBER THAT a cat needs affection, too, and your help. Sit still, and it will come, seeking that warm, comforting lap it has not entirely forgotten. Be there to open the door for it.

Realize that all dog owners go through this, and few find it easy. I miss the little boy who insisted I watch "Full House" with him, and who has now sealed himself into a bedroom with a stereo and TV. The little girl who wrote me mush notes and is now peeling rubber in the driveway.

> The only consolation is that if you do it right, let them go, be cool as a cat yourself, one day they will walk into the kitchen and give you a big kiss and say, "You've been on your feet all day, let me get those dishes for you." And you'll realize they're dogs again.

7-13

Category	Cat	Dog
Apology	What are you talking about!	will initiate even when not at fault

A dog's commitment to harmony is endless. They want peace and cohesiveness. If there is a rift between people, the dog will volunteer to initially contact the different parties and seek resolution via an apology. The cat is often oblivious to the fact that there is a rift. It is more accurate to say that cats and dogs have a different degree of sensitivity as to what is a rift. Boxing illustrates cats and dogs' sensitivities. In boxing, it is a violation to hit an opponent "below the belt." This is because the person is too vulnerable below the belt line. So too, everyone has an invisible emotional belt line. The difference is that dogs have a much higher emotional belt line—they are more sensitive about more things. The cat has a much lower belt line and lacks the awareness of others' belt lines. What is a playful banter to a cat may feel like a hurtful slight to a dog.

Vignette: Apologize?

While at the company picnic, Cathy and Devon had an incomplete interaction that could be best described as awkward. From an outsider's viewpoint, the exchange affected Devon much more than Cathy. Devon stewed about it all night, so that Sunday morning's coffee didn't even produce alertness. By noon, Devon phoned Cathy. To assist the dialogue he opened with, "Cathy, if there was anything on my side that caused any ruffles, I want to apologize." Even though Devon thought Cathy was clearly at fault, he had hoped that by generously opening with the preface, the call would allow Cathy the opportunity to apologize.

Cathy's reply of, "Devon, I didn't even think twice about that conversation," resulted in Devon being even more confused. He felt doubly awkward. He hadn't done anything at the picnic, yet he was the one apologizing.

Having recovered from Cathy's response, he tried again: "Sometimes things are said that have nothing to do with what is currently going on. Are there any burrs under your saddle that we need to talk about?"

Cathy said, "Devon, obviously you have reflected on this a lot more than I have. Nothing comes to mind."

Within a minute they were off the phone. By mid afternoon Devon was emotionally disheveled enough that his wife sat him down and asked what was wrong. During the ensuing probe, Devon realized that there was a pattern of Cathy slighting him and being unaware of having done so.

7-14

Category	Cat	Dog
Decision-making process	loves to decide	would rather only gather info

One of the easiest ways to know how groups assign value to its cat and dog members is to view group dynamics during the decision-making process. The decision-making process is made up of four phases:

Gathering	Evaluating	Deciding	Implementing

For our purposes, the correlation between a *cat*, an individual who has a *credible* voice pattern, and an individual who operates from *position* is so high the terms are interchangeable. The cat's credible voice is interpreted by others as sending information. Likewise the correlation between a *dog*, an individual who has an *approachable* voice pattern and an individual who operates from *person* ais so high that those terms are interchangeable. The dog's approachable voice is perceived as seeking information.

During the Gathering phase, the more pertinent information found, the better. The *approachable* voice person is an asset, because such a voice pattern elicits more information. During the Deciding phase, the *credible* voice tends to exude the definitiveness that is often held in esteem. It is no small coincidence that the male's guttural voice and the rhythmic nature of the female voice add to the cultural perception that females elicit more information than males do. Conversely, males are seen as more definitive. Time and time again, the roles that males and females have played in meetings reinforce these points. The flow of information[43] is greater if females are facilitating.[44]

Decisions are reached more quickly when males are chairing. John Gray, in *Men are from Mars, Women are from Venus*, and Deborah Tannen, in *You Just Don't Understand*, are saying that the modern male is allowed, and even at times encouraged, to switch from the *credible*-sending information pattern to the *approachable*-seeking information pattern. Such switching actually adds to their gender appeal. These are "Sensitive, New-Age-Guys." Our society still doesn't have many accolades or positive descriptions for the female who switches from the *approachable*-seeking information pattern to the *credible*-sending information pattern.

One way to predict which participants will be valued during each phase is to study the voice patterns of the players. Cats have *flat voices with intonation that curls down* and are labeled *credible* (⟍). Dogs speak with a *rhythmic voice with intonation that curls up* and are termed *approachable* (∧∧ʃ).

Culture

7-15

From a group dynamics standpoint, if the cats' *credible voice* dominates during the Gathering phase, that phase is quickly left and the Evaluating and especially the Deciding phase is entered. In the cat culture that over-emphasizes the *credible* voices, the group is quick to arrive at a decision. Whether cats have gathered the appropriate information is always questionable. The more the committee is composed of high-level positions (e.g., district office personnel), the more this pattern occurs.

For cats, saving time is often more important than the validity of the decision.

Gathering	Evaluating	Deciding	Implementing
credible-oriented people			

If the dogs' *approachable* voices are valued and actively present during the Gathering of Information, this phase lasts longer and more information is obtained. The dog culture which favors the approachable end of the voice continuum tends to procrastinate entering the next two phases for fear that the decision might offend or impose upon individuals.

Gathering	Evaluating	Deciding	Implementing
approachable -oriented people			

The dogs don't want to move out of the gathering phase. This is because when they get ready to evaluate and decide on a course of action, they think of one person who might be adversely affected by the decision. In contrast, cats rush to the evaluating and deciding phases. People who can handle pressure with ease, such as the responsibility of deciding, are promoted and given more challenges.

In groups where voice patterns indicate that both *credible* cats and *approachable* dogs are actively present, the dogs are highly sought during the Gathering phase and disregarded during the Evaluating and especially the Deciding phases.

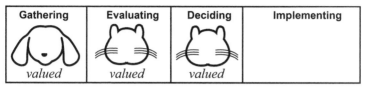

Gathering	Evaluating	Deciding	Implementing
valued	*valued*	*valued*	

Neither dogs nor cats are good at making decisions. The dogs aren't good at it because they shy from deciding or because they are ashamed of what they have finally decided and they worry about how badly others are affected by their decisions. The cats are so busy with the next set of decisions they are making that they don't have time to check how the last set of decisions was carried out. As Peter Senge says, we don't know the effect of our actions.[45]

Vignette: The Four Phases

Barbara discovers during her annual check up that she has a medical condition that warrants her phasing out of her CEO position. Behind closed doors, she negotiates a surprise maneuver with the board. She will remain the titular head so that she maintains veto power while her two vice presidents actually run the company.

Carl welcomes the increase in power, while Donald has to be reassured that he is worthy of such advancement. To balance Carl and Donald, Barbara promotes Devon, a *dot*, as Carl's special assistant and Cathy, a *cag*, as Donald's special assistant. Devon is strong enough to withstand Carl's pressure and Cathy is gentle enough to listen to Donald's self-deprecating style. Barbara whisks all four away to a sequestered retreat. She opens the retreat with a quote from Hewlett-Packard's Paul Henderson:

"Value only gets added when people exchange information or when they make decisions. Plenty has been written about how to share information and very little about making decisions."

Barbara explains that every day they will be engaged in decision-making processes. The four phases of the decision-making process are: Gathering, Evaluating, Deciding and Implementing information. It is imperative that they understand whether a cat or dog will be valued during each of the phases. The major questions to focus on are:

- How do groups of cats handle the decision-making process?

- How do groups of dogs approach the same process?

- When both cats and dogs comprise the group, why do the cats dominate disproportionate to their numbers?

She expounds the concept, "It's obvious why cats are promoted more than dogs. In fact, the initials of an *Executive Director - E D -* are the same as the initials for the second and third phases of the decision-making process: *Evaluating* and *Deciding.* These two skills, evaluating and deciding, are the most essential skills for you to be successful leader.

"If, however, you want to be a charismatic leader, you grow to understand that dog people live by the golden rule of treating others the way they want to be treated. Dogs have excellent manners or can be easily trained to have them. When a group of dogs engage in the decision-making process, they share the invisible microphone. If one says to another, 'How are you?' the one who has been asked will immediately ask in return, 'And how are you?' Implied in the Golden Rule is that others will treat you the way you treat them—which is true for dog people but not for cat people.

"To lead cat people, charismatic leaders move beyond the Golden Rule to the Platinum Rule: treat others the way they need to be treated. Always have something the cat wants. Sometimes this is achieved by just being weird. The trick is to seem normal to the dogs while being perceived as different by the cats."

Barbara ends the retreat on the difference between garden-variety leaders and charismatic leaders by presenting two computer-generated pictures. The picture of Carl has the right side of his face composed of Devon. The photo of Donald has his left facial side be that of Cathy.

Chapter 7 Reflections: The concepts of *position-pilot* and *person-flight attendant* (page 108) add synonyms to our *cat* and *dog* dictionary:

- In what situations am I a cat / pilot and when am I a dog / flight attendant?

- In which situations can I just be myself and which ones do I intentionally need to be more flexible?

The timing of our intervention as managers depends on the culture of the group (pages 119-122):

- What is my style and does it innately fit with the culture(s) I operate in?

- How does the quote, "It is dangerous to manage from my dog persona" apply to me?

Understanding "Apology" (page 128) helps the dog part of me to not be personally offended by unaware cats:

- Which obtuse people in my world do I feel hurt by?

- Where in my world might I be oblivious to hurting others?

Parting Pets

***A charismatic leader has both high expectations
and high relationships.***

Charisma the Art of Relationships is a blueprint for developing charismatic leadership through relationships. This work draws parallels to behaviors that are surprisingly analogous to those observed in pets. There is nothing intrinsically good or bad about the cooperative and compliant nature of the dog or the independence and often unawareness of others of the cat. Context determines the appropriateness of behaviors. I want to be flexible in developing personal relationships with dogs and working relationships with cats. I also want to know how to preserve those relationships when managing.

P-1

Any time a set of behaviors is labeled, there is the danger of generalization. Obviously, people are complicated. They are neither *all* cat nor *all* dog. At the same time, behavioral models assist us in recognizing the patterns of communication. *Charisma* suffers the disadvantages of generalizations and yet, as a well-tested model, it helps us know what to expect in interactions and frees us from the danger of being constantly surprised by life. Behavioral models increase our ability to form and maintain relationships with a wide variety of people.

P-2

The exercises in this book are tools for becoming a powerful leader, one who exudes charisma. They are part of the author's work on non-verbal intelligence— the ability to recognize, label, predict, and respond

P-3

appropriately to patterns of communication. Leaders with non-verbal intelligence are proactive. Effective communicators know what is likely to happen *before* it happens; therefore, they have more options in handling challenging situations and relationships.

P-4

For example, if I am involved with a committee and can recognize the animal composition of that committee, I know what is likely to happen. I want to be attentive to my relationships with different members as well as the relationships amongst the members. That way, I can predict who is likely to dominate this meeting. Is the domination helpful or not? If not, by adjusting my behaviors, I influence the outcome. Reality is more complex than generalizations, so I want to stay alert to those attending each meeting.

Since dogs and cats come in many varieties, it is useful to consider the cat and dog analogy as a continuum.

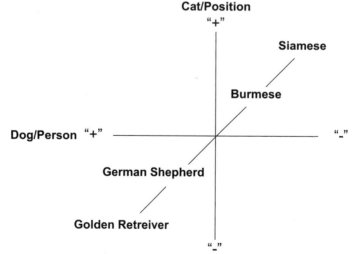

The Golden Retriever lives to please. We don't expect them to protect us. The German Shepherd is mostly dog with some cat traits and lives to protect. If you don't have enough space for a dog and yet still want a pet that fetches, get a Burmese. They are mostly cat with some dog traits.

We place individuals on the continuum based on the person's cat-like and dog-like behaviors. People who are closer to the dog end will exhibit more dog-like tendencies. Forming a relationship with them is easy. Give them what they want—a personal relationship with you. Give them direct attention and thank them for their loyalty and dedication. Because you appreciate them, they will follow your leadership. No need to command them—just ask for a favor and they will love the opportunity to give back to you.

Likewise, people closer to the cat end will be more cat-like. Forming a relationship with them is more challenging. Give them what they want—which isn't us. Is it prestige? Limelight? Position? Notoriety? Expertise? Once you know what they want, indirectly give them part of it. Teasing strategies have the most effect on them. It doesn't help to command them—they don't recognize anyone as superior to them.

P-5

As interesting as it is to place an individual on the continuum, the real benefit of the analogy is found when we ask, "What is the distance between where one individual is and the location of the person he is interacting with?"

P-6

The ones closer to each other get along better because there are less distinct cat and dog roles. Those farther apart from each other will compare to their animal counterparts.

P-7

For instance, a Golden Retriever will be compatible with a German Shepherd; the German Shepherd will also get along well with a Burmese cat. Don't ask about the Siamese with a Burmese. The Siamese doesn't know that anyone else of importance exists. Even a cat may become dog-like in the presence of someone who is much more cat. (Witness the iron-handed vice president who becomes meek and submissive when the CEO cat pays a visit.)

The implications of this are profound. Since I have both a cat and dog part of me, I can access a variety of behaviors. If my normal location is distant from another's location on the cat-dog continuum, we are likely to have difficult times communicating. By changing how I behave, I can promote my own success as well as the success of the groups I belong to. Instead of demanding by power, I influence through relationships. I am able to be more understanding, get along better with others, and utilize their strengths.

Power and Influence

> *We are inadvertently in love with*
> *the influence of power.*
> *And we need to be in love with*
> *the power of influence.*

When readers reflect on the cat and dog concept, they usually gravitate toward the dog descriptors. There are two reasons for this, both flowing from the strengths of dogs. Most of us want to be liked and most of us prefer to operate from influence.

Dr. Warren G. Bennis, president of Stanford, captures the disappointment of someone who is finally promoted to the highest rung of the corporate ladder: "I realized an important personal truth. I was never going to be completely happy with positional power, the only kind of power an organization can bestow. What I really wanted was personal power, influence."[46]

A vision of a world managed by influence inspires us. John Lennon's song "Imagine" epitomizes this hope. However, management by influence is not enough. Lasting success depends on the presence of power in the background.

P-8

So an individual can have a lot of influence, perhaps as a liaison of the organization or an indispensable resource for the health of the group. And yet, in order to have true charisma, the person still has to have the backup of authority and the willingness to use power when needed. Charismatic leaders primarily operate from influence; moreover, they are comfortable switching to power when the situation warrants it.

Management by influence requires the backing of a disciplinary system that is clear, consistent, and known. One of the fastest ways to destroy management by influence is for top management to not support a manager's occasional use of an appropriate threat or disciplinary action. If support from above is absent, the rungs below operate in a void. Uncertainty causes havoc.

Influence plus power (used judiciously) is charisma.

P-9

Learning

While the exercises in this book are tools for becoming a charismatic leader, each of us selects the level of charisma we want. When people expand their repertoire, there is a learning curve. Initially we feel awkward. We do not feel like we are being ourselves. This is especially true when learning how to select the appropriate level of cat and dog-ness. After practicing a new skill for a while, the behavior feels more familiar and we begin to redefine ourselves.

To become charismatic, dogs have to give themselves permission to practice positional authority and credibility. Cats have to become humble and vulnerable, let their person out, and practice approachability.

There is a story that brings laughter and comfort to us as we learn to expand our self-image. Charlie Chaplin, the famous silent film actor, was vacationing at the French Riviera. The Mediterranean resort where he was staying was hosting a Charlie Chaplin look-alike contest. He entered and came in third place.

P-10

Balance—My Relationship With Myself

Many of us may have initially read this book about charisma and relationship and thought of our professional world. We are all affected by our own or others' style of leadership. We may also have surprised ourselves as we find benefit in understanding our relationship with ourselves better—especially our deep need for love and intimacy. (Study the genealogy chart on page 15.)

Each person has cat aspects and dog aspects. We balance our lives when we have contexts that support letting both our cat and our dog out. This balance is easier when the persona elicited at work is different from the one who comes out at home. If, at work, we are mainly a cat, then we want to come home and recharge ourselves by increasing our dog. No matter how valued we are for being problem solvers at work, our partner at home wants to love a vulnerable human being. Fixing things at home makes us appreciated, not lovable.

It might be hard for the perfectionist cat to allow others to do household chores. It might be hard for them to bite their tongue when a task is not done to their standards. It might be hard for them to resist the temptation to redo the job. And yet, it is imperative the cat does so. A cat experiences greater freedom in knowing that excellence doesn't require perfection, and humility really is a virtue. Being able to come home and set their burdens down, taking the mantle of responsibilities off their shoulders and experiencing an exhale, are essential for greater health.

Some of us operate mainly as a dog at work. By increasing our cat at home, we have a realm where we are the lead. We can exercise our ambitions and feel empowered. We can lead with knowledge, skills, and status.

Gail and I are co-entrepreneurs. We live on a eight-acre tree farm. One of the best things we have ever done is to move the office out of our home. We converted our lawnmower shed into our headquarters. The thirty steps from the back door of the home to the front door of the office is a journey between two worlds. In the office, I am the lead—innovative and often random. I love to explore, dream, and wonder "What if?" Gail is steady and makes order out of the chaos that I create. Gail stabilizes processes, does fulfillment, and has a customer service voice that welcomes those phoning. In the home, we reverse roles. Gail is totally creative in the kitchen. We don't have meals; we have her latest artistic dish. She is a cooking cat—she experiments the most when company is coming. I am content to vacuum and wash dishes.

> *If you are a dog, lucky enough to find*
> *a way of life you love,*
> *we wish you courage to feel worthy to live it.*
>
> *If you are a cat, ingenious enough to carve out*
> *a way of life you love,*
> *we wish you vulnerability to share it.*[47]

End Notes

(The page on which the end note appears is listed in parentheses. Our intention is to cite the origin of quotes and concepts. If you discover an inadvertent oversight on our part, please contact us at www.michaelgrinder.com.)

1. (p. 1) Walker, Donald. (1996) *Never Try to Teach a Pig to Sing...Wit and Wisdom for Leaders*. San Diego, CA: Lathrop Press.

2. (p. 2) Unknown. If you know the source, please inform us so we can give credit.

3. (p. 3) Unknown. If you know the source, please inform us so we can give credit.

4. (p. 4) Unknown. If you know the source, please inform us so we can give credit.

5. (p. 6) Dentinger, Ron. (August, 2000) in Dodgeville, Wis., Chronicle. *Reader's Digest*.

6. (p. 18) The movie (1995) is based on the *Biography of President Harry S. Truman* by David McCullough.

7. (p. 28) *History of Niagara Falls*. William "Red" Hill, Sr. 1888-1942. Famous Niagara River daredevil. During his lifetime he was the recipient of four Royal Humane Society medals for acts of bravery.

8. (p. 31) David Livingstone, 1813-1873. Scottish missionary, explorer. He extensively explored central Africa and exercised a formative influence upon Western attitudes toward Africa.

9. (p. 32) George Will, ABC News Commentator and syndicated columnist, Pulitzer Prize winner.

10. (p. 35) We ask Irish fans to assist us in tracking

down this source so that credit can be given.

11. (p. 43) Grinder, Michael. (2007) *The Elusive Obvious (The Science of Non-verbal Communication).* MGA Publishers, Battle Ground, WA pp. 46-63.

12. (p. 49) Powell, Colin and Persico, Joseph. (2003) *My American Journey.* New York: Ballantine Books.

13. (p. 51) Developed with Tim Dalmau (Australia).

14. (p. 52) Anthropologist Patricia Phelan, mentioned during a private conversation, Spring, 2003, Portland, Oregon.

15. (p. 53) Mentioned to me by a fine Indian business man while riding a trolley in London.

16. (p. 55) Grinder, *The Elusive Obvious* pp. 66-68.

17. (p. 56) Grinder, *The Elusive Obvious* pp. 80-84.

18. (p. 57) George Miller. (1956) "The Magical Number Seven, Plus or Minus Two" in Psychological Review.

19. (p. 58) Grinder, *The Elusive Obvious* pp. 164-165.

20. (p. 59) Fisher, Roger and Sharp, Alan. (1998) *Getting it Done.* New York: Harper Business, p. 32.

21. (p. 60) Bateson, Gregory. (1972) *Steps to an Ecology of Mind.* The University of Chicago Press.

22. (p. 63) Famous scientist and science fiction writer.

23. (p. 64) When I read a stranger in my seminars, the individual and the group are amazed. Now for the first time in print, this section of *Charisma* explains my methodology for detecting a person's style or thinking, the kinds of people the person does well

with, and most especially how I respectfully reveal the person's deeply-held values.

24. (p. 65) Joseph Luft discusses the Johari Window in his book (1969) *Of Human Interaction*. NY: National Press Books. The model is modified for the specific purposes of this work.

25. (p. 68) Developed by Becky Herndon and Seth Morris.

26. (p. 71) All contributions are welcomed: North County Community Food Bank (NCCFB), P.O. 2106, Battle Ground, WA 98604 (360) 687-5007.

27. (p. 72) "A friendly voice" is composed of a rhythmic undulation that curls up at the end of phrases and sentences.

28. (p. 72) "A businesslike voice" is composed of a flat voice tone with an intonation that curls down at the end of phrases and sentences.

29. (p. 81) A corporate term for a lower position effectively influencing a superior.

30.   (p. 84) People tend to get promoted past their level of competence.

31. (p. 84) Frank Scully.

32. (p. 86) Diane Sawyer, ABC News Prime Time Live.

33. (p. 86) Kouzes, James M. and Posner, Barry Z. (1993) *Credibility*. San Francisco: Jossey-Bass Publishers.

34. (p. 89) Fisher, Roger and Ury, William. (1981) *Getting to Yes*. New York: Penguin Books.

35. (p. 95) I have misplaced the research. We appreciate assistance on the source or an equivalent one.

36. (p. 105) Walker.

37. (p. 108) Powell and Persico.

38. (p. 117) Grinder, *The Elusive Obvious*, pp. 84-85.

39. (p. 118) *A Few Good Men*, 1992, Columbia Pictures.

40. (p. 122) As quoted in John Gottman's (2001) *The Relationship Cure*, p. 174. New York: Crown Publishers.

41. (p. 123) Tuckman, Bruce. (1965) "Developmental Sequence in Small Groups" in *Psychological Bulletin*.

42. (p. 126) Adair has two $10 books: *Welcome to Earth, Mom* and *At Adair's House*, 97 Scott St., San Francisco CA 94117.

43. (p. 131) One of many sources is Herrmann, Ned. (1993) *The Creative Brain*. Lake Lure: Brainbooks.

44. (p. 131) Gray, John. (1992) *Men are From Mars, Woman are from Venus*. New York: Harper Collins. Tannen, Deborah. (1990) *You Just Don't Understand*. New York: Ballantine Books.

45. (p. 133) Senge, Peter. (1990) *The Fifth Discipline*. New York: Doubleday Current.

46. (p. 141) Bennis, Warren G. (1997) *Managing People is Like Herding Cats*. Provo UT: Executive Excellence Publishing.

47. (p. 144) For viewing pleasure see the 1996 movie, *Truth About Cats and Dogs*, directed by Michael Lehmann.

Bibliography

Bateson, Gregory. (1972). *Steps to an Ecology of Mind.* The University of Chicago Press.

Bennis, Warren G. (1997). *Managing People is Like Herding Cats.* Provo, UT: Executive Excellence Publishing.

Covey, Stephen R. (1989). *Seven Habits of Highly Effective People.* New York: Simon & Schuster.

Fisher, Roger and Sharp, Alan. (1999). *Getting it Done.* New York: Harper Business.

Fisher, Roger and Ury, William. (1983). *Getting to Yes.* New York: Penguin Books.

Gottman, John. (2001). *The Relationship Cure.* New York: Crown Publishers.

Gray, John. (1992). *Men are From Mars, Woman are from Venus.* NY: Harper Collins.

Grinder, Michael. (2013). *The Elusive Obvious-The Science of Non-Verbal Communication* (3rd ed.). Battle Ground, WA: MGA Publishers.

Herrmann, Ned. (1991). *The Creative Brain.* Lake Lure: Brainbooks.

Kouzes, James M. and Posner, Barry Z. (1993). *Credibility.* San Francisco: Jossey-Bass Publishers.

Lara, Adair. (1996). "When Children Turn Into Cats." *San Francisco Chronicle.*

Luft, Joseph. (1969). *Of Human Interaction.* New York: National Press Books.

Miller, George. (1956). "The Magical Number Seven, Plus or Minus Two" in *Psychological Review*, p. 63.

Powell, Colin and Persico, Joseph. (2003). *My American Journey*. New York: Ballantine Books.

Senge, Peter. (1990). *The Fifth Discipline*. New York: Doubleday Current.

Tannen, Deborah. (1990). *You Just Don't Understand*. New York: Ballantine Books, Inc.

Tuckman, Bruce. (1965). "Developmental Sequence in Small Groups" in *Psychological Bulletin*.

Walker, Donald. (1996). *Never Try to Teach a Pig to Sing*. San Diego, CA: Lathrop Press.

Wheatley, Margaret. (1992). *Leadership and the New Science*. San Francisco: Berrett-Koehler Publishers.

The Big Cat—Effective Strategies*

"The Big Cat" focuses on the challenge of dealing with the Big Cats in our professional lives. It is a challenge because our skills have to be practiced and our definition of success sophisticated. At the same time, dealing with cats is a fine opportunity because once their loyalty is gained, that loyalty is often greater than a "dog's" loyalty; and besides, they will kill our rats. Their loyalty is worth the effort required to foster a working relationship with cats…even the big cats.

First, a summary of some *Charisma* strategies, then some advanced strategies. For most of us, dealing with the cat is both a challenge and an opportunity.

Charisma Strategies

We use the strategies found in this book, namely:

Two-point vs. Threepoint Communication (page 76)

If the content is positive, then making eye contact is fine (two-point). If the content is volatile, then looking and pointing at the information on a paper is suggested (three-point). However, even if you offer the information in the third point format, the larger issue is how to get the cat to consider you as worthy enough to offer.

Catnip: Pause and Look Intelligent (page 54)

Since cats are attracted to quality, the more intelligent you appear to the cat, the more likely it is that you will have

---

*Special thanks to Sharon Sayler and Hazel-Ann Lorkins for contributing.

permission to offer the third point communication. To appear intelligent to the cat, do the following:

1. When listening and you are standing, keep your forearms in one of the following three postures:

   • both forearms at your side,

   • or both forearms parallel to the ground (optional: lightly clasping your fingers in front of your waist),

   • or a combination of one forearm at your side and the other parallel to the ground.

2. When talking via third point with volatile information, pause frequently with a frozen hand gesture. Keep your head, lips, and gesture still until you are ready to speak again.

Pause and Look Intelligent mesmerizes the cat. Since the cat doesn't know why he is attracted to your delivery, he is even more intrigued... and cats love to be intrigued.

Profiling (page 69)

Telling a cat something about himself that is not public knowledge intrigues the cat. This is especially true when the level of insight is mental habits and thinking styles. The cat internally muses, "Well, if you know this about me, what else do you know that you are not telling me that would be helpful?" The cat is very interested in improvement. If you are a source of insights that result in the cat's improvement, you could be given the key to the cat's city.

Decision-making Process (page 39-45)

Recognize the phase that the decision-making process is in and adopt the physiology that is appropriate. During the gathering phase, be more dog, flight attendant, and approachable, and use two-point communication. During the evaluating and deciding phases, shift your non-verbals to cat, pilot, and credible, and use three-point communication. This will keep you as a valuable contributor throughout the process.

Calibration (page 72)

Adapt the cat's style. Cats don't like softeners such as *may, might, could, perhaps*. Cats don't have time for tap dancing. Say what you mean and mean what you say. And for heaven's sake, get rid of wanting to be liked. Realize that the cat doesn't have to like you for your interactions to be effective. As a university president once remarked, "If you want approval, get a puppy."*

At the same time, recognize when the cat is showing a crack in his credible veneer and match it by being a pinch more vulnerable. Yet, don't be surprised when the cat suddenly slams the door to his sanctuary.**

Linguistic Neuro (page 77)

When you need information that is not forthcoming, make several statements that could be the information you need. Pause after each statement. The statement that the cat reacts to is the door that has powerful information behind it.

Advanced Strategies

Congruency (page 60)

Dogs and small cats respond well to the strategies just mentioned. Big cats disdain "gimmick strategies" unless they are

---

*Walker p. 46
**A great scene in "The Devil Wears Prada" illustrates this point.

done with high congruency and great comfort. Congruence is displayed with our control of our own non-verbals, our non-blinking delivery, and emotional comfort as evidenced by our abdominal breathing.

Focus on Yourself

Essential to successfully working with a big cat is resisting our urge to control, manage, or change the cat an improbable task. Instead, we focus on controlling, managing, and changing our self. For example, we control when and where we look. We control our voice pattern, our posture, and our gestures. Most importantly, we control our breathing; we stay relaxed. The extent to which we can control our self determines how likely it is that we will we be able to influence the cat.

"Eyes Wide Open" (page 61)

To operate with the big cat, we have to modify the axiom, "Use a third point when delivering volatile news." Cats want us to look them right in the eye and say what needs to be said." The cat is impressed when we do eyeball-to-eyeball communication with congruency without blinking. Here why.

The average human blinks six to eight times a minute when talking. Typically, humans blink to access the next set of words/concepts they want to say. By memorizing what we want to say ahead of time, we increase our ability to deliver a message with our eyes wide open. The cat won't consciously know why it is impressed with you, and that delightfully fascinates the cat. Hey, a real cat sleeps 20 hours a day—our congruency wakes the cat up. You have something that the cat can't identify but wants, and that makes the cat even more intrigued.

There are some sophisticated byproducts of the non-blinking technique. (Oh, how cats love anything that has the word, "sophisticated" associated with it.)

1. We mentioned previously that the frozen hand gesture during a pause kinesthetically holds the listener's attention and that moving the gesture during the pause detracts from the quality of the message. A blink is the visual equivalent of the gesture moving during the pause. Learn to keep your eyes open when talking to a cat.

2. The cat seeks the highest level of development possible. Competition helps the cat to such heights. Cats sharpen their own tools by engaging with high quality opponents. This explains why trial attorneys can go head-to-head with each other in court and then afterwards socially go out with each other. At a boxing match, during the introduction the two fighters are nose to nose as the referee recites the rules. Neither boxer blinks. Keeping your eyes open is interpreted by the cat as, "This is a worthy opponent."

Abdominal Breathing (page 57)

We know we are comfortable when we breathe low. What might be the reason for us not breathing low? Usually, high breathing shows a lack of permission with our self. Most of our interactions with reality are a reflection of our inner reality. How much permission do I give myself when using the various strategies? If I am breathing high/shallow when using the strategies, my permission with myself is low. Literally, I am negotiating with myself in front of the cat; I am asking myself, "Am I really comfortable doing this? Have I stretched myself too far outside my comfort zone?" When I breathe high/shallow, the cat may well be reacting to my own incongruence instead of responding to the strategy. Cats have a good nose for smelling uncertainty; our ambivalence allows the cat to eat us for breakfast.

To increase our ability to breathe low and keep our eyes wide open, we rehearse what we want to say ahead of time. We practice several variations ahead of time so our flexibility will be greater.

We need to understand the mechanics of abdominal breathing. When you are breathing abdominally, notice how the *exhalation* elongates. When you are breathing from high in the chest, notice how the *inhalation* elongates. By practicing how to breathe abdominally with an emphasis on exhalation, you will prepare yourself for future situations with cats. Why does this work? It's because the needs optimum oxygen to function at its highest level. With plenty of oxygen, we are more relaxed, able to listen, think, and respond. Besides the benefits to ourselves that abdominal breathing provides, there is an effect on big cats—the cat will be duly impressed with us. It is our new sense of confidence that the cat respects.

You can practice abdominal breathing by lying on the floor, back against the wall, and bending over like athletes do during timeouts.

Having experienced abdominal breathing in a structured posture, the trick is to maintain this breathing while upright, while talking, and while moving. By holding one forearm parallel to the floor with your hand in front of your mid section, you'll notice that each expansion and contraction of the abdomen pushes the forearm farther away or closer to the body. Feeling your forearm move is a feedback system indicating you are breathing low.

Another suggestion is to stand in front of a mirror and see what abdominal breathing looks like. Abdominal breathing isn't the most flattering view of oneself (so much for vanity), but accepting a slight paunch is a small price to pay for effectively working with a cat. Truthfully, the cat won't notice.

Ask a Question

When interacting with a cat that is your superior, it is wiser to ask a question than to make a statement. Sometimes we find ourselves in a situation where the boss is about to implement a decision without having all the pertinent information. Yet you wonder if the boss is receptive to necessary information—things you know that he doesn't know. To increase the boss' openness to information, you have to access the cat's values. For example, if the boss values prestige then, "We certainly can carry out that decision. The larger concern is if enough information has been gathered to insure that this decision will add to your reputation rather than detract."

An example of answering a question is the scene from "The King and I" where one of the king's wives approaches the English school teacher and informs her that foreign dignitaries are coming and the king would appreciate assistance on how to appear modern. The teacher replies, "Oh, so he wants me to tell him how to act." The wife rushes to reply, "It must not sound like that."

Asking Questions that Access the Cat's Values

Instead of making statements that the cat can dismiss, offer structured questions. The structure accesses the cat's highest held values. Structure the question so that the cat is in a bind with herself.

For example, Sally has eight people who report to her. She is about to launch a project that would have three of these subordinates working side-by-side. On a "competency" level the teaming makes sense. However, you know that the dynamics will likely be troublesome. You know that one of Sally's highest values is her belief that because she has been with the company longer than anyone else, she knows how to be successful. You might structure your question, "Sally, you have formed more teams than anyone else in the company. What, *besides competency,* is needed to make a team operate successfully?"

Your question does two things. First, you have hooked her into her pride of experience with the wording, "…formed more teams than anyone else…" Secondly, the question takes away her "ready" answer of "competency." If you can "leave" the question with her, the question's poignancy is increased. After the question is presented, don't be present so that she has to think instead of speak. Examples would be leaving a message on voice mail, sending an email, or asking the question as you are leaving her presence. For example, "Sally, I am late for my 11:00. The next time we are together, I want to ask your advice. You have formed more teams than anyone else in the company. Besides competency, what is needed to make a team operate successfully?" Then you leave immediately.

Asking Questions that Force the Cat to Go Outside Itself

Cats are self-selective; they decide their own reality. This includes deciding what is important and relevant. Often a cat needs to consider information and perspectives that we have, but the cat arrogantly believes it already has the needed information and that it knows what is best for others. The cat is oblivious to external reality. We need a work around.

There is a great example of this in the 2007 movie, *The Queen*. The prime minister of the UK wants the queen to acknowledge Princess Diana's passing. The queen has been adamant that Diana's death is a private matter—not something that the royalty need to engage in. During a pivotal scene, she says to Tony Blair, "I doubt there is anyone who knows the British more than I do...." Wisely, Tony started that conversation and subsequent conversations with, "Have you seen the papers today?" Instead of the dialogue being between the queen and the prime minister, Tony is using the newspapers as a third point. The external evidence of the newspaper finally leads the queen to question herself as the best source of knowing what her people need.

The equivalent in everyday life is to ask someone who is not likely to budge from a preset belief the following series of statements and questions. "There are two possible approaches we can operate from. You are very clear that (*mention the possibility favored by the cat*) is endorsed by you. The other possibility is (*mention the alternative*). What external, observable evidence would appear that would support the first possibility? And, equally important, what is the external, observable evidence that would support the second possibility?"

Accessing Heroine

Since cats invented arrogance, they tend to bristle at any hint that others expect them to contribute to a common cause. However, the cat is equally prone to want to ride the white horse to rescue people. So the next time you need a cat's assistance, one strategy is to say face-to-face, "This project doesn't have a ghost of a chance of being successful without your support and contribution." Similarly, "We are hurting. The project is at a standstill. It can only be resurrected if you would be generous enough to...." Simply, you have switched the focus from the cat being a contributor to a *common* cause to the cat being an *uncommon* contributor.

My sister talks to college presidents by explaining a project and then saying, "But it will never work." After a long pause, she adds in a whisper, "...unless, of course, you decide that it is worthy of your attention."

"You Would Know Best."

Sometimes we don't have the luxury of "asking a question," because by duty we need to speak up and make a statement. Using the preface of, "You would know best" in front of the suggestion allows the cat to focus on the suggestion. Otherwise, the cat might not be listening because he is preoccupied with, "Who does this person think she is...?" and more importantly, "Does this person know who I am?"

"You would know best" can be used with anyone who thinks they are superior to us. The person's perception of his superiority might be based on age, gender, education level, experience, wealth, ethnicity, nationality, accent, or success.

Preface your remarks with, "You would know best," then say what you were going to say. The preface acknowledges the listener's self perception of superiority. In using "You would know best," you are taking care of the issue of superiority so that the focus can be on the content of your message.

Index

Charisma—The Art of Relationships Live from London, DVD and Audio Album

Spend 1-1/2 hours with Michael as he entertainingly applies his cat and dog analogy to a wide array of applications. Topics include raising teenagers, understanding how to manage difficult personalities, increasing the efficiency of committee meetings and developing presentation skills. Michael's engaging style, humorous anecdotes and poignant insights will have you both laughing and reflecting at the same time. Sold as DVD & Audio Album (Album includes a Bonus CD of Charisma Worksheets and Screen Savers.) Also sold separately.

A Cat in the Dog House

ENVoY has struck a nerve in the educational community around the world. The book has been translated into six languages. The purpose of the **ENVoY** program is to preserve relationships with students during management. The demographics of the classroom have changed. Increasingly, students seem to resist the teacher's attempts to form a relationship. Michael's *A Cat in the Dog House* addresses this dilemma and retools educators with successful strategies to form working relationships with these hard-to-reach students. Sold as an Album of 4 DVD's and 4 CD's or sold separately. Also available as an eBook.

Avoiding a Cat Fight - Successful Parent Conferences

Teachers are more familiar and comfortable with students than parents. Educators are win-win people. This eBook provides the tools to recognize and respond to hostile parents. You will gain a perspective that lets you keep your cool when interacting with anger.

Parenting UFOs - More than Surviving Adolescence

UFO stands for Unidentifiable, Formerly Ours. Join Michael as he shares techniques, methods and approaches that gives you sanity when your off-spring are off-the-scale. You will laugh and cry as you realize you are DOING OK when they are not. Sold as an eBook.

The Elusive Obvious - The Science of Non-Verbal Communication

Brimming with practical ideas you can try today, *The Elusive Obvious* reveals the twenty-one non-verbals that are found at the heart of all communication models, no matter how different they may appear on the surface. This ground-breaking book explores the roots and mastery of non-verbal behaviors that make up 90% of all communication. The non-verbals presented form the foundation of influence and success in communication. *The Elusive Obvious* products include: Book, eBook, DVD, Laminates, Flash Cards, and Album.

Visit our website www.michaelgrinder.com

Schedule of Michael's classes. Latest announcements. Sign up for free email quote of the day. Free worksheets. Additional products.